Essentials of Financial Risk Management

Essentials of Financial Risk Management

Practical Concepts for the General Manager

Rick Nason
Brendan Chard

BUSINESS EXPERT PRESS

First published in 2018 by
Business Expert Press, LLC
222 East 46th Street, New York, NY 10017
www.businessexpertpress.com

ISBN-13: 978-1-94709-838-1 (paperback)
ISBN-13: 978-1-94709-839-8 (e-book)

Business Expert Press Finance and Financial Management Collection

Collection ISSN: 2331-0049 (print)
Collection ISSN: 2331-0057 (electronic)

Cover and interior design by S4Carlisle Publishing Services
Private Ltd., Chennai, India

First edition: 2018

10 9 8 7 6 5 4 3 2 1

Printed in the United States of America.

Abstract

Financial risk management is a growing field of specialization in business. With the increased level of regulation and emphasis on financial reporting, the role of the financial risk manager has never been more prominent. This book covers the concepts, tools, and techniques of financial risk management in a comprehensive, yet easy-to-understand manner. Avoiding academic jargon wherever possible, the book has as its objective to be a rigorous, yet practical guide to financial risk management.

This book is intended for senior managers, directors, risk managers, students of risk management, and all others who need to be concerned about financial risk management or who are interested in learning more about this growing career path.

Keywords

decision making, enterprise risk management, financial risk management, hedging, regulation, risk management, risk mitigation, strategic analysis

Contents

Acknowledgments

We have both been very fortunate to have worked in risk management with many very talented people. To them we owe a debt of gratitude for our risk management educations as well as helping each of us to develop a passion for risk management.

We would also like to thank our respective families for their understanding and patience as we spent many an hour away from them in order to complete this book.

Introduction

Why a New Book on Financial Risk Management?

There are lots of books on financial risk management—why the need for this one? It is a very fair question. The reason we are writing this book is that we believe there is a need for a book on financial risk management for the rest of us; those of us who are not quantitative geeks, those of us who do not want to wade through a large number of formulas, those of us who do not want to deal with abstractions that take away from the real-world applicability of much of the world of risk management. In other words, a concise, yet thorough book on what one needs to know to be effective (rather than just knowledgeable) about risk management.

Financial risk management is managing the volatility and uncertainty of financial prices. In our ever-increasingly connected and global business landscape, managing the financial risks of a firm is more important than ever and perhaps more difficult to do properly. The good news is that there are lots of tools, tactics, and techniques for doing so. The not-so-good news is that many of these techniques are being developed for the quantitatively inclined, rather than for the practical business manager. This is the gap that this book aims to narrow significantly by providing a no-nonsense guide to the essentials of financial risk management.

Financial risk management has been an important aspect of corporate management probably since financial transactions replaced bartering as a mechanism for trade. There is evidence that early form of derivative contracts existed in biblical times, and in more or less continuous use since then. Financial risk management has continued to evolve, but a modern transformation took place when Fischer Black, Myron Scholes, and Robert Merton developed the Black-Scholes Merton option pricing model in the 1970s. Financial risk management exploded into the public conscience for all the wrong reasons as derivative debacles of the late 1990s led famed investor Warren Buffet to call derivatives "weapons of financial mass destruction". Of course, derivatives, or more specifically

Collateralized Debt Obligations and Credit Derivatives, again became front page buzz words during the financial crisis of 2008 as risk management techniques again seemingly not only failed but backfired.

This is, however, not a book about financial derivatives—although derivatives and derivative concepts frequently do play a role in financial risk management. This book is a common-sense approach for managing the day-to-day financial risks that come about from operating in our ever-increasingly connected and global world. At a time when focus on implementing a competitive strategy is as important as ever, no firm is safe from having their well-thought-out plans derailed by unexpected volatility in financial prices. Failure to properly manage financial risks generally leads to failure or at least a damaged reputation of the managers and the directors. That being so, it is incumbent upon managers and directors to have a firm grasp of risk management principles and to effectively develop and implement an appropriate risk management strategy.

The aim of this book is to cut through the clutter and get to the essence of best practices in financial risk management. It is a book based in theory but focused on practice and being practical in its approach. It is a book for those who need to practice financial risk management, rather than theorize about financial risk management. It is not a "Dummies" book. It is a book for the intelligent and thoughtful manager who wants to as efficiently as possible gain the financial risk management knowledge and know-how necessary so they can get on to their foremost job of managing their department or even the firm.

Who This Book Is Intended For

This book is first and foremost for practitioners. It is intended for those managers who understand the importance of financial risk management for the achievement of their goals. While the manager may not actually be implementing the financial risk management tactics themselves, they realize the importance of knowledge of the principles so they can intelligently integrate their operational strategies with the financial risk management strategy. Knowledge of risk management strategies allows one to implement strategies with a higher degree of confidence with a lower probability of derailment due to unforeseen financial events.

The book is also a useful primer for the general manager who wants to expand their skill set. Financial risk management knowledge is increasingly necessary for senior managers. If one aspires to senior management, then financial risk management is a key piece of the skill and knowledge set needed.

The original impetus for this book was the increasing demand for training for Boards of Directors that we encountered. Financial risk management expertise is not a nice-to-have feature, but instead it is a necessity for Board members. In recognition of this, Chapter 10 on Risk Governance has a section dedicated to the specific issues that Board members need to pay attention to.

This book is also a practical guide for the investor who wishes to learn more about financial risk management in the goal of making better investment decisions. An understanding of a firm's financial risk management practices can certainly help an investor build a much better risk adjusted and performing portfolio. Understanding a firm's risk management strategies not only helps identify when a firm may be exposed to unwanted adverse moves, but also provides insight into economic situations where a firm may be particularly well positioned competitively.

This book, particularly when combined with its sister books (*Rethinking Risk Management: Critically Examining Old Ideas and New Concepts,*[1] and *Essentials of Enterprise Risk Management*[2]), forms the basis for a comprehensive course in risk management. We have used the materials for this series of books in MBA-level courses and Executive training seminars and corporate training programs for several years. Students appreciate the practical yet rigorous approach as contrasted with the dry academic style of many other financial risk management texts.

Finally, the book is also suitable for other stakeholders such as regulators, lawyers, or accountants who need a concise yet comprehensive practical understanding of financial risk management.

---

[1] R. Nason. 2017. *Rethinking Risk Management: Critically Examining Old Ideas and New Concepts* (New York, NY: Business Experts Press).

[2] R. Nason and L. Frade. 2018. *Essentials of Enterprise Risk Management.* (New York, NY: Business Experts Press).

A Few Central Tenets

Before concluding this Introduction, we would like to mention the six central tenets of this book that will be covered in depth in Chapter 1 and which form the basis of our philosophy of financial risk management. These tenets are: (1) firms (with the exception of financial institutions) are not in business to take financial risk, (2) deciding not to hedge a financial risk is still a hedging decision, (3) hope is not a prudent financial risk management strategy, (4) the appropriate definition of risk is that risk is the possibility that bad or good things may happen, (5) the only perfect hedge is in a Japanese Garden, and (6) financial risk management is a value-added activity.

Perhaps the most significant tenet of this book is that financial risk management is a value-added activity. It is our aim to have you, the reader, believe that taking the time to go through this book was indeed a value-added activity.

CHAPTER 1

The Importance of Financial Risk Management

What Is Financial Risk Management?

Financial risk management is managing the financial variables that affect the firm. It is an ongoing and continual process of identifying financial risks, assessing their potential for harm or opportunity, making a decision of the best managing technique, implementing the chosen risk management strategy, assessing the effectiveness of the strategy, creating a communication network and an associated level of transparency about the risks, and developing impactful risk management reports.

Financial risk management incorporates a set of tools, metrics, and best practices that have been developed over time. Although financial risk management is well developed as a practice, it remains in practice as much of an art as it is a science due to the nature of risk itself.

Financial risk management is a key component of successfully managing a company that has financial exposures, which includes almost any profit-oriented company. Financial risk management is not just a "nice to have" activity, but instead should be considered a necessity. In fact, it is increasingly becoming an expectation of all publicly traded companies. Additionally, it is imperative for senior managers and directors of these companies to familiarize themselves with the tools, techniques, and tactics of financial risk management. Knowledge of financial risk management and an understanding of the role it plays in the competitive success of a company are imperative for good corporate management and governance.

It is important to note that risk is two-sided; it can be either positive or negative. The definition of risk that we use is that "risk is the possibility that bad or good things may happen." This of course is slightly different from the lay definition of risk. However, financial variables can move in favor of the organization; a key supply commodity can fall in price, interest rates can fall and decrease interest costs and increase demand for a firm's products, or currency rates may change so as to make a company's products more price competitive in other countries.

There are three elements to our working definition of risk: (1) risk is about the future, (2) risk has an element of uncertainty, and (3) risk has an upside and a downside to it. Thus, financial risk management is a forward-looking activity that one needs to be aware of and must be flexible enough to deal with uncertainty, and financial risk management needs to manage both good risk and bad risk. It is the last element that often gets neglected in risk management. All too frequently, risk management is focusing on managing the downside risk, while not seeing, and thus not taking or capturing, sometimes even more significant upside risks. Effective financial risk management applies to managing both bad risk and good risk.

Why Is Financial Risk Management Important?

In the last two decades, a wide variety of advanced-level university programs in financial risk management, risk engineering, or risk mathematics have been developed. Additionally, various organizations and certification programs devoted to the field have become popular among practitioners and those wishing to enter this dynamic profession. Most corporations, particularly those with international scope, have organized a dedicated financial risk management department, often including a C-level executive. Of course, this has always been the case for financial institutions, whose reason for being is to manage financial risk, but the prominence of financial risk has also become of almost equal importance in nonfinancial corporations.

There are a wide variety of reasons as to why financial risk management has become so prominent. One of the primary reasons is the globalization of the economy. The rapidity of the rise of globalization has not only increased the level of competitiveness, but also dramatically increased the connectedness of economies. Globalization means that it is no longer sufficient to be the best managed company within your specific home piece of geography, selling products and services to a dedicated and loyal client base. Today's customer is global, and so is today's competition. As such, global economic factors and financial markets have the potential to tip the playing scale to one's advantage or disadvantage. Labor rates, exchange rates, different tax regimes, and differing access to and cost of raw supplies can gain one a competitive advantage or put one at a significant competitive disadvantage. Without the ability to manage these factors, an organization is leaving itself at the whims of the economic Gods and, more importantly, in the crosshairs of their competition who do gain the ability to manage these financial risks.

Also related to globalization is the connectedness of markets. What were once isolated risks, confined to either one specific sector of the market, or one part of the global economy are now events that tend to become globally systemic. This, of course, was most clearly seen during the 2008 financial crisis when basically all major markets globally suffered massive losses in unison. In a global environment, where potentially no one is safe, the need for risk management is key for long-term survival and competitive advantage.

The connectedness of the markets leads to the concept of emergence, which is a fundamental property of what is known as complex adaptive systems. Emergence is a phenomenon that is observed not only in a wide variety of biological systems, but also in economic systems. Emergence explains how fads and feedback loops get started, as well as stopped. Many economists use emergence as an explanation for stock market bubbles and crashes, for the volatility of commodity prices, and for changes in consumer demand for goods and services. A fundamental property of complex adaptive systems is that we can observe trends and patterns after the fact, but are hopeless in our ability to predict them. We will have more to say about complex adaptive systems later in this chapter, but for the moment it is important that the increasing complexity of the global economy increases both the need for and the value of proactive financial risk management.

Awareness of risk management techniques has developed its own kind of feedback loop leading to increased adoption. The rise of financial products for trading financial risks starting in the late 1970s with the emerging markets for future and option contracts led to the development of bespoke over-the-counter products for virtually every financial risk imaginable in the 1990s. That development has continued to the present-day scenario where financial engineering as well as the emerging "fintech" technologies have made the ability to manage financial risk ever more sophisticated, yet ever more accessible to even the leanest of companies. With this increased accessibility to financial risk management products and techniques has come an increased expectation that companies will make use of financial risk management know-how.

Stakeholders expect companies to have a view on financial risk management and to implement that view with the appropriate financial risk management tactics and products—even if that view is that financial risk should not be managed by the company, but by the stakeholders themselves. Stakeholders in an organization are increasingly demanding that the firm develop and communicate a clear risk management philosophy and for them to consistently implement risk management tactics that are consistent with that philosophy. This is a point that we will discuss at length in Chapter 10 when we discuss risk management governance.

Increasingly, corporate stakeholders do not like to be surprised by corporate results that are affected by financial risks that could have been hedged away; with the possible exception of a few select type of companies that explicitly and consciously desire to have their corporate valuation subject to the whims of the financial markets or commodity prices. Share price volatility causes lower share valuations and higher debt financing costs (ironically, a result that is a function of advances in quantifying and managing credit risk). Credit agencies in particular have developed financial models that illustrate how credit ratings, and the associated probability of default, are based on financial share price volatility. Banks routinely make the financial risk management practices of corporations a major part of the credit analysis process, and frequently incorporate specific financial risk management practices as one of the covenants before granting a loan.

Regulators are another group of stakeholders who closely monitor the financial risk management practices of a company. Many industries voluntarily and preemptively implement best practices of financial risk management to avoid having more rigorous risk management imposed on them by regulators. Regulators frequently rely on financial risk management metrics as a way of assessing the viability and the compliance of the firm. This has led to compliance being an integral part of the financial risk management agenda.

Customers and suppliers do not like surprises caused by a lack of appropriate financial risk management practices. Fluctuating prices and shortages of supply can destroy whatever goodwill that a company develops with its customers. Conversely, creatively using financial risk management techniques can provide a competitive advantage in both attracting new customers and keeping existing customers.

Case Study

Irving Oil

Irving Oil is an integrated energy company headquartered in Saint John, New Brunswick, which through its subsidiary Irving Energy, provides customers, both industrial and retail consumers, a "Price Cap program" which it describes as follows:

> With Irving Energy, you can cap your home heating rate for 12 months! With Cap Pricing, you pay a small fee to ensure that your price will never go higher than the capped price. But should prices go down, you get the benefit of paying the lower price.

This is analogous to buying a call option: you pay a premium and are protected if market prices rise, but retain the benefits if prices fall! This type of contract provides access to hedging options for many companies without the sophistication or desire to trade financial products on their own. The customer now knows that regardless of how high market prices go over the next year, they will never have to pay more than the agreed-to price cap. This increases their budgeting and forecasting abilities, increasing the probability of meeting financial objectives. The 12-month term offered by Irving is quite standard, and does not provide any protection from rising market prices beyond the following year.

An often neglected stakeholder group that might be one of the most impacted by inappropriate financial risk management is the employees, and by extension the future employees, of the organization. There is the obvious impact of the company going bankrupt. Other major concerns exist though beyond the existence of the company and its related job security. Many employees have share ownership programs. Excessive levels of stock price volatility impact them directly in the value of their personal portfolios. Perhaps, the biggest impact is value volatility of pension programs. As the baby boomers begin to retire, underfunded, or excessive volatility in pension plans will become more exposed and make companies more vulnerable in the war to attract talent.

An industry of training for risk management expertise has developed to supply managers the expected expertise. What was once considered to be esoteric and solely for the specialist is now common place. For instance, back in the early 1990s, swaps were considered a novel and hard-to-understand product. They were new, novel, and cutting edge. Now swaps are covered in virtually every undergraduate business program as part of the core curriculum, and are considered as mundane a product of risk management as a calculator might be. During the 2008 financial crisis, products such as credit derivatives and highly structured collateralized debt obligations, more commonly known as CDOs, were likewise considered esoteric, but it is likely that their use will someday be seen as common. Today, we have fintech products such as blockchain and cryptocurrencies that are new and novel. These tools are already changing the financial risk management landscape in profound ways and new developments will continue to emerge.

It is not just knowledge of the risk management products themselves that is important. It is also an increasing awareness of the tools, tactics, and measures of risk management. Everyone, from Board members to the newly hired employee, is expected to be familiar with a range of financial risk management topics. Awareness has created an expectation. It has also created a demand for risk management educational opportunities, as well as professional certifications. Two of the major risk certification programs are the Professional Risk Manager designation, offered by the Professional Risk Manager's International Association (PRMIA), and the Financial Risk Manager designation granted by the Global Association of Risk Professionals. To meet the demand, Universities are creating specialized degree programs in financial risk management and financial engineering.

Ultimately, the major stakeholders in financial risk management are the managers themselves. Higher volatility of stock prices, particularly when caused by hedgable risks, is seen as a sign of ineffective management, and thus careers and career progression are at stake for managers whose financial risk management skills are not competitive. Even mid-level managers need to be aware of how financial risks can affect the achievement of their operational goals, and failure to understand the risks and to manage them is considered inexcusable and potentially career limiting.

Strategic Importance of Financial Risk Management

A common misperception is that financial risk management is simply about controlling the volatility of costs, prices, and credit risk. Financial risk management ultimately has its biggest virtue in being a major element of implementing the strategic plan. The hedging strategy of the firm has a direct role to play in not only setting, but also implementing a strategic plan for competitive advantage. How an airline chooses to hedge its fuel costs also helps to determine the pricing strategy relative to its competitors. The pricing plans a company offers its customers, based on its own financial risk management, can become a comparative advantage in the eyes of its customers. Mining companies can decide whether their value is based on their effectiveness of mining commodities, or based on the value of the commodities they mine on the basis of their financial risk management strategy.

Thus, for many companies, financial risk management has relatively little to do with the direct financial results and a lot more to do with implementation of the strategic plan. In those companies, financial management is truly value-added and a source of competitive advantage. An effective financial risk management strategy allows for a much wider set of alternatives for the strategic vision of the firm. Financial risk management becomes a catalyst and an enabler for strategic management.

Types of Financial Risk

There are six major types of financial risk, and a few specialty classifications as well. Although there are similarities in how each of these types of financial risk is managed, there are also specific differences between them.

There are different measures for risk in each of the markets, as well as specific market dynamics that need to be accounted for in how the financial risk management products work in each of the markets.

Perhaps the most prominent financial risk is interest rate risk. It is the risk that arises through changing interest rates. Interest rate risk affects not only financing costs, but also potentially affects demand for a firm's products or services. Of course, interest rates also affect the overall economy, which affects all companies. Consider for a moment the effect of interest rates on the demand for housing, automobiles, and other high-ticket consumer items. However, effective financial risk management can mitigate the negative effects of interest rate changes and likewise help the firm leverage advantageous changes in interest rates.

The second most prominent financial risk for managers to be concerned about is currency risk which arises through changes in exchange rates between countries. Currency risk is closely related to interest rate risk as it is directly tied to the relative interest rates between countries. It is a common misperception that currency risk is only an issue for organizations that have international operations or sell their products internationally. However, in the global economy, all companies are affected by currency risk as it changes the relative competitiveness of foreign competitors and foreign substitutes. If the domestic currency strengthens relative to the currency of a competitor, then the domestic competitor will be at a relative price disadvantage solely due to the changes in exchange rates. Of course, exchange rates will also affect the price of commodities and perhaps even the price of substitutes. Exchange rates can also ripple through an economy, significantly impacting trade balances and overall economic growth. Thus, currency risk can be a company-specific risk, an industry-specific risk, or even a country-wide systemic risk.

Volatile energy prices are a constant concern as well. Energy risk management in particular has some specific risk management issues. Energy is a commodity that cannot be transferred digitally, unlike an interest rate or a currency. Energy is also a local product, and thus the price and availability of electricity in Texas can differ quite substantially from the price in New York, for instance, if a storm has knocked out the transmission capabilities in the area.

Credit risk can arise in many different forms. It is most often associated with the risk of a specific company having a credit event such as bankruptcy. However, credit risk can also be systemic as was observed during the financial crisis when credit availability was extremely difficult to find regardless of the financial health of a firm. Companies that did not manage their credit risk adequately found themselves scrambling to source even short-term credit. Even highly rated General Electric was rumored to be facing a significant credit crunch during the worst moments of the crisis.

Commodity risk is the risk that the price of commodity inputs, or the sale price of commodities will change. Commodity prices can be affected by a wide variety of factors and can be particularly volatile. Commodity risk is probably the financial risk that has been managed for the longest period of time. It was mentioned earlier that there were indications that derivatives were used to hedge agricultural products during biblical times. Markets for the trading of commodities are the oldest of the exchanges.

There are a few other risks that, while strictly speaking are not financial risks, are sometimes included with financial risks as related products and tactics for managing them exist. Two such products are weather risk and catastrophe risk. Weather risk is the risk involved with changes in weather patterns and catastrophe risk is associated with major events such as tornados or floods.

Ultimately, all financial risks become strategic in nature. Effective management of these financial risks can lead directly to long-term strategic advantage. Of course, the converse is also true in that ineffective management of financial risks can lead to a strategic disadvantage.

Financial Risk Management Tenets

Throughout this book, we will rely on a few central tenets that will guide the discussion. These tenets form a solid basis for understanding the potential role that financial risk management can play in an organization's success.

Firms Are Not in Business to Take Financial Risk

With the obvious exception of financial institutions, and some commodity trading and mining firms, corporations are generally not in business to take financial risk. They are in business to create and market products and services. That is their competitive advantage, and that is what they should stick to. If they believe that their expertise is in predicting financial prices, then they should become a hedge fund or a trading firm. Implicitly we know of many firms that act like a hedge fund. They confuse prudent financial risk management with activities that are more in line with financial trading. It almost always ends poorly.

This is not to say that nonfinancial firms should never take a view on the markets and adjust their risk management techniques accordingly. However, if more focus is put on forecasting financial prices than making and marketing products, then there is a serious strategic risk management issue within the company.

Ironically, firms often unintentionally slip into actively taking financial price risk through the hedging they do for their financial risk management program. The risk management activities make a profit, which of course in a proper hedging program means that the firm had an associated and offsetting loss in its operations due to the move in financial prices. Some firms, however, fail to commingle the gain from their hedging program with the changes in the cash flows from their operations. They jump to the incorrect conclusion that if they made profits from doing a little bit of hedging that they should thus do more hedging. They proceed to expand their hedging program without an offsetting increase in the size of their operations. This means that the size of their hedging activities is out of balance with the size of the financial risk associated with their operations. This imbalance is essentially taking a speculative view on the financial markets. It is something that we strongly caution against. In large part, this is what sparked many of the corporate derivatives debacles. It is a case of using a very valuable tool much too aggressively and in a way that it is not intended.

Firms are in business to provide a product or a service. They are not in business to take financial risk.

Ignoring or Being Unaware of a Financial Risk Is Still a Risk Management Decision

Ignoring or being unaware of a financial risk is still a risk management decision. It is simply not a good financial decision. Many companies claim that they do not believe in hedging financial risks because they consider it too difficult to do so. We believe that this is a preposterous decision and a shameful decision as well.

A risk management program does not need to be sophisticated. Likewise, developing a basic knowledge of the financial risks that a firm is exposed to is not difficult. Indeed, it is true that some companies do build elaborate risk management models and implement incredibly advanced plans for financial risk management. However, much value can be gained from just the simplest of risk management tools.

We will argue that, like with any other organizational tactic, financial risk management practices can be taken too far. Choosing the appropriate level of financial risk management for an organization, however, is not hard to do. The common sense and intuition of the Board and the senior management team should be able to make a decision on this.

There is simply no adequate excuse or reason for a firm to choose to ignore or be unaware of financial risk and financial risk management practice. The only time that an organization should ignore a financial risk is when they have extensively analyzed it and come to the conclusion that the risk is not sufficient to warrant the effort to manage it, which in some cases is the prudent and proper decision.

Hope Is Not a Prudent Financial Risk Management Strategy

Related to deciding to remain ignorant of financial risks is the strategy of hoping that financial risks will go in your favor. It sounds silly, but "hoping" is the strategy implicitly adopted by many firms. With the availability and ease of use of tools for prudent financial risk management, it is almost unethical and certainly irresponsible for managers to rely upon hope as the basis of their risk management. Hope is obviously not a prudent financial risk management strategy.

Financial Risk Management Is as Much an Art as It Is a Science

The advent of educational programs and certifications for financial risk management has made it seem as if financial risk management was some type of science on a par with physics or mathematics. In fact, many of the participants in these financial risk management programs come from a background of mathematics or physics (and in the interests of full disclosure, so do one of the authors of this book).

Risk management is based on uncertainty and probability.[1] This implies that we are ignorant about the specifics of what will happen in the future. Mathematics, however, is based on axioms that are always true and predictable (one plus two will always be equal to three) and physics is based on the laws of nature (an apple will always fall to the ground when dropped on earth and will not randomly float upward). So although we are constantly trying to make risk management seem more like science, there is a limit to how far we can go with this. Risk has a fundamentally different character than science.

In our experience in risk management, we have seen a growing separation between what we call the "gray hairs" and the "mathematicians." The "gray hairs" have significant experience and intuitively understand how the financial markets work. The mathematicians know advanced analytical techniques and can quantify probabilities of outcomes of risk management strategies. Both have something to offer in developing risk management ideas. Ignoring the mathematical ideas of risk management means that one will miss out on a lot of powerful tools and ideas. However, it is equally true that ignoring the intuition of risk managers who have experience in how the markets work means also ignoring very valuable insights and ideas.

Great risk management involves both the art and science of the discipline. Ignoring one at the expense of the other will always lead to suboptimal results, and perhaps even financial disaster.

The Only Perfect Hedge Is in a Japanese Garden

As just stated above, risk management is about the future and uncertainty. It is simply not possible to have perfection when one makes plans for the uncertain future, and thus risk management is as much an art as it is a science.

---

[1]You may believe that using the terms probability and uncertainty in the same sentence is redundant. In the theoretical risk world, the two have quite different meanings. Probability implies that we have a mathematical formula to calculate the odds that something will happen and that we know the range of outcomes. For instance, if I flip a fair coin, then I know there is a 50-percent probability that it will land heads up and a 50-percent probability that it will land tails up. Uncertainty implies that you do not know the range of outcomes possible. For instance, I cannot predict what the most popular consumer product will be 50 years from now because it is not possible to forecast the range of new products that will be developed in that time period.

Furthermore, even with the benefit of hindsight, which of course is not possible, risk management tradeoffs and compromises will need to be made. There is no perfect plan, and there is no risk management plan that does not involve compromises. There is no perfection in financial risk management. An old adage of risk management that we certainly buy into is that the only perfect hedge is in a Japanese Garden. The flip side of this is the equivalently true adage that it is better to be approximately right than be precisely wrong.

Risk Management Is Complex

Earlier in this chapter, we discussed complex adaptive systems and its central property of emergence. Complex systems and emergence come about when agents (for example, starlings in the sky, fish in the ocean, or people in an economy), can interact and also when they can change their behavior. Thus, we get murmurations of starlings, schools of fish, and stock markets bubbles and busts—all of which are examples of emergence, and all of which demonstrate that we live in a complex world.

Complex systems are contrasted with complicated systems. Complicated systems run by the axioms of mathematics, and the laws of science. They are completely predictable and they are also completely reproducible. We can fire a missile with incredible accuracy. We can plot the orbit of the planets in minute detail for decades to come. We cannot, however, predict what financial prices will be next week, much less next month. That is the difference between complex systems and complicated systems. We can see patterns in complex systems, but only with hindsight. We have no ability to forecast complex systems.

Management of complicated and complex systems requires very different skill sets. In part, this comes back to the art and science of risk management. In part, it is the reason why there are no perfect risk management solutions. As big data, and artificial intelligence, and as more people get trained and certified as risk management "scientists," it is important to remember the difference between a system that is complex and something that is complicated.[2] Risk management is complex.

---

[2]For the reader interested in learning more about the role of complexity in business, a suggestion is R. Nason. 2017. *It's Not Complicated: The Art and Science of Complexity in Business* (Toronto, Canada: University of Toronto Press).

Financial Risk Management Adds Value

Despite the lack of perfection, a properly designed and implemented financial risk management plan does add value to the organization. Although most risk management strategies come with a cost, which may be an explicit cost and/or an implicit cost, the benefits of risk management almost always outweigh these costs in the long run.

One of the direct benefits is that financial risk management lowers financing costs. Financial risk management also leads to lower stock price volatility, which in turn leads to higher valuations. However, there are also many indirect benefits of financial risk management. It leads to more stable costs, which in turn allows the firm to offer more stable prices. Financial risk management allows managers of the firm to concentrate on the operational tasks that they can affect, rather than what is happening in the global financial markets which they cannot affect. This leads to better management performance, which in turn leads to better organizational performance. Ultimately, prudent financial risk management leads to peace of mind.

Financial risk management is a value-added tool that should be exercised by virtually firms in some way, shape, or form.

Concluding Thoughts

Financial risk management is not a "nice to have" activity, a luxury for large corporations, or something that can be ignored by a company without explicit interest rate, currency, or commodity risk. Financial risk management is imperative for every organization that has financial stakeholders.

While financial risk management does involve some advanced tools, techniques, and admittedly some advanced mathematics, the reality is that the basics of financial risk management can and should be understood and practiced by all managers and directors. It is an activity of the firm that adds significant value and greatly improves the achievement of the strategic objective of the firm.

CHAPTER 2

Financial Risk Management Tools and Tactics

Responses to Risk

Before beginning a discussion of the various tools and tactics used to manage financial risks, it is instructive to review the range of possible responses to financial risks. It is appropriate to realize that there is a range of responses to risk: eliminate, avoid, mitigate, ignore, embellish, and embrace.[1] These responses range from weak (mitigate, embellish) to neutral (ignore), to strong (eliminate, embrace), and also reflect the philosophy that risk can be positive as well as negative. Just as the responses to risk have a range, so too do the financial risk management tools. Furthermore, just as it is important in any type of craftsmanship to choose the right tool for the task, so it is in financial risk management.

Part of choosing the tool for risk management depends on whether the risk is predominately a negative risk, or predominantly a positive risk. Not always, but generally in financial risk management, a risk that is a negative risk for one organization is a positive risk for a different organization. A second component is understanding the side effects, or the unintended consequences of a risk tool. An old saying about financial risk management is that the "only perfect hedge is in a Japanese Garden." Virtually all risk tools either have an explicit cost or some unintended consequence that renders the risk tool as less than perfect. That is simply the nature of risk management. That is not to say that one should not use risk management tools, but one does need to know

---

[1]This list is from R. Nason and L. Fleming. 2018. *Essentials of Enterprise Risk Management* (Business Experts Press), New York.

the respective advantages and drawbacks of the various tools available to the risk manager.

Operational Financial Risk Management Strategies

There are several operational strategies for managing financial risk. For instance, operations can be designed to offset currency risks; financing can be arranged to minimize interest rate risk; sales contracts can be set to reduce commodity price risk. The way an organization chooses to implement its operations can provide a wide variety of risk benefits.

The design of both the revenue and the cost structures of the firm is the place to begin when considering operations as part of the risk plan. Different operational implementations can be used to either increase or decrease financial risks. Therefore, it is only prudent to consider alternative operational strategies as part of the overall risk management plan.

For one example, strategic placement of manufacturing plants is one basic strategy to reduce currency risk. With manufacturing and costs in the same currency as sales creates a natural offset where the currency exposures are set at a minimum. This is a very blunt tactic if used solely for risk management, but also one that has a host of other advantages (closer to market, potentially easier logistics, political protection against trade barriers) and disadvantages including significant direct and indirect costs (increased amount of assets tied up in plant and equipment, increased managerial supervision, lessening of economies of scale). Not only is it a blunt instrument, but it is also one that generally cannot be quickly altered or changed if the strategy of the company changes. Although a powerful tool, it is obviously one method for financial risk management that needs to be carefully considered and likely one that would not be chosen solely for reasons of financial risk management.

A simpler and more flexible way to accomplish much of the same financial risk mitigation as opening a foreign plant is to source financing in the same currency as sales will be. A company can finance in one currency and then convert the currency to the currency of the home country. This creates a revenue stream in a foreign currency (the foreign currency where the sales are being made), as well as an offsetting liability in that same currency (due to the sourcing of financing in the foreign currency).

If the foreign currency depreciates, then net revenues calculated in the home currency will likewise decrease. However, the depreciation of the foreign currency also implies that the interest payments, and repayment of the loan in the foreign currency, will also decrease in value, relative to value in the home currency. This creates a natural offset. The offset will not be perfect as the sales revenue will likely not be equal to the value of the loan payments, but it is a good base from which to start a hedging program. This strategy can also be done synthetically using currency swaps and this will be discussed in Chapter 6.

Another similar strategy is to outsource the form of manufacturing that is causing the financial risk, whether it is currency risk or commodity risk. By outsourcing production which has, for instance, commodity price risk, under long-term fixed price contracts, a company effectively is shifting the price risk to the supplier. While doing so reduces the commodity price risk, it also reduces flexibility in manufacturing capability.

Similarly, a company can outsource its price risk for commodity inputs by setting up agreements with third-party sources for supply of commodity inputs at prearranged fixed prices. For instance, a Canadian company that uses oil as an input to its manufacturing could enter into a long-term fixed price deal with a fuel supplier to purchase oil at a fixed Canadian dollar price over a 5-year period. Such a contract would both fix (and thus hedge) the price of oil, as well as fix (and thus hedge) the exchange rate risk between the Canadian dollar and the U.S. dollar as oil is sold denominated in U.S. dollars. Again, this strategy involves shifting the price risk onto the suppliers, who likely will charge more for providing this implicit service, but even given a different cost structure it may be beneficial to do so on the basis of the risk management benefits.

Operations integrated with risk management can also be used for marketing advantage. For instance, a company could provide the option to its global clients to choose the currency in which they wish to pay. In essence, by offering fixed prices, in a variety of currencies, the company is giving a free currency option to its customers. Some clients will take advantage of this by timing their purchase to advantageous changes in exchange rates. Other clients will be thankful that they do not have to worry about the currency risk. Either way, the company can use this simple tactic to increase sales. Of course, this increases the currency risk for the company, but this currency risk can be offset using other financial risk management techniques. If the company is comfortable managing currency risk, the costs of doing so should be more than offset by the advantage given to the clients.

Effectively automobile companies do something similar when offering long-term leasing and borrowing rates at attractive fixed rates to its potential customers. The auto manufacturers, all of whom have advanced financial risk management capabilities, essentially manage the interest rate risk so clients can put their focus on buying new cars, rather than on what the fluctuation of car payments due to changing interest rates might be in the future.

Several different oil companies employ this strategy for heating fuel in Northern climates. Fluctuating fuel costs can be a major source of worry for home consumers of heating oil. Furthermore, the cost for fuel oil tends to be correlated with colder temperatures, so an especially cold winter could do serious harm to a family's household budget; the colder it is, the more fuel oil they will require, and the higher the fuel price will tend to be. To counteract this and gain a marketing advantage, fuel companies will essentially offer a fuel price cap. For agreeing to pay a few pennies more per gallon of fuel oil, the fuel company will "cap," or provide a maximum price for which fuel prices will rise over the winter months. In essence, the fuel company is offering its customers the choice to purchase a call option on fuel prices. The fuel company manages its increased price exposure to its own fuel costs, but provides peace of mind to its customers and has a significant marketing story to tell in its advertising.

When one thinks of managing financial risks, one generally does not think of managing them through strategic use of operational activities. However, operations can provide a very effective long-term baseline for managing a variety of financial risks. Furthermore, operational activities can be used to increase or decrease risk levels. Therefore, prudent risk managers will consider operations a key tool in their risk management toolbox.

Financial Tools

Introduction to Derivatives

When most people think of financial risk management, they think of using financial derivatives. Financial derivatives are a very efficient risk management tool. However, as with most tools, they can produce unintended consequences if used improperly, or without a full understanding of what they can and cannot accomplish.

A derivative in general is nothing but a contract that is entered into today that has a value that is based on the value of something in the future. For example, a currency option depends on the future exchange rate between two currencies, or a forward rate agreement depends on the realized interest rate at some specific point in the future. Derivative contracts are available on a wide variety of financial assets, such as interest rates, exchange rates, commodity prices, financial assets, and even the weather!

We can break financial derivatives into two basic types: forward type derivatives and option type derivatives.

A forward is a contract where the two counterparties agree today on a mutually binding price at which they will transact on a future date for a given quantity of an underlying asset. The buyer of the forward contract agrees to buy at the prespecified price, while the buyer agrees to sell at the prespecified price. There is no upfront cost or premium to enter into a forward agreement since the "forward price" is set so that it is a fair trade to both of the counterparties.

For instance, a company that uses oil in their manufacturing process may enter into a forward contract to purchase 1,000 barrels of oil in 6 months' time at a price of $50 per barrel. If the price of oil rises above $50, they still pay $50 per barrel, and likewise if the price of oil is less than $50 in 6 months' time, they still pay $50. In essence, the company has "fixed" their purchase of oil prices at $50 per barrel for the amount of 1,000 barrels.

An option contract is similar except that the buyer of the option contract has the right but not the obligation to transact at a given price in the future for a given amount of the underlying asset. The seller of the option contract has to transact whenever the buyer of the option "exercises" their option to transact. A call option gives the buyer the right (but not the obligation) to buy at a preset price called the strike price, while a put option gives the buyer the right (but not the obligation) to sell at a preset strike price. To have the flexibility to have the right but not the obligation to transact means that the buyer of an option pays an upfront premium to the seller of an option. Option contracts have more flexibility in design than forwards, as the preagreed-upon price to transact in the future can be set at different levels for which the size of the upfront premium can be adjusted to account for the different expected values to the two counterparties to the trade. In a forward contract, which does not involve an upfront payment, the forward price of the transaction needs to be set at inception at a level that is "fair" to both counterparties. Thus, there is one price at which a forward contract can be set, but there can be a wide range at which the "strike price" for an option can be set, as different strike prices will imply different option premiums.

For example, our manufacturing company instead of entering into a forward contract as a method to hedge their oil purchase may decide instead to pay $4 per barrel for a call option which gives them the option to buy 1,000 barrels of oil in 6 months at a strike price of $50 per barrel. If in 6 months' time oil is selling at a price above $50 per barrel, then the company will exercise their option to buy the oil at $50. However, if the price of oil is trading at less than $50 at the time that the option matures, then they will choose not to exercise their option to buy at $50 from the counterparty, but instead will buy in the open market at the prevailing cheaper price. The option buyer thus is hedged against adverse price moves (oil prices going up in our example), but also gets to benefit from advantageous price moves (oil prices going down in our example).

In essence, our manufacturing company has "capped" the price they will have to pay for oil, while a company that has entered into a forward contract has "fixed" the price at which they will pay. Of course, the option has an associated upfront premium that offsets this advantage. This is a fundamental difference between forward style contracts and option contracts.

A put works the same way except that it provides a minimum price, or a "floor" on the value of an asset. For instance, a small gold producer may be concerned that gold prices will fall before they can mine their planned gold production in the next 3 months. To protect against falling gold prices, the miner could buy a put to sell 1,000 ounces of gold in 3 months' time at a strike price of $1,200. Assume the premium for this is $10 per ounce, or $10,000 for all 1,000 ounces. If in 3 months gold is trading at a level above $1,200, the gold producer will not exercise their option to sell at a price of $1,200, but instead will sell at the prevailing higher market price. However, if at the time of maturity of the option the price of gold is below the strike price of $1,200, then the gold producer will exercise their put option and sell at the strike price of $1,200.

Options give the option buyer flexibility in that they allow the buyer to profit from advantageous price moves, while protecting against adverse price moves. Forward contracts "lock-in" the price. With a forward contract, the hedger is protected against adverse price moves, but does not have the opportunity to benefit from advantageous price changes.

Choosing between Doing Nothing, Hedging with a Forward Contract, and Hedging with an Option Contract

To illustrate the differences between not hedging and hedging with forward contracts and option contracts, it is helpful to consider a simple example. Assume that a purchasing manager needs to purchase a given commodity in 3 months' time. The purchasing manager is concerned about rising prices for the commodity. The manager has three basic alternatives open to them; they could do nothing and buy at the prevailing price in 3 months' time; they could enter into a forward contract to buy the commodity at a forward price of $100; or they could pay $10 and buy a call option to have the right but not the obligation to buy the commodity at a strike price of $100 in 3 months' time.

Figure 2.1 below gives the level of "satisfaction" that the purchasing manager has with their strategy, given a reference point of $100.[2] The first column of the table shows possible prices for the underlying commodity in 3 months' time. The second column shows the value of the "do nothing" strategy, while the third and fourth columns show the relative value of the buy forward strategy and the buy call option strategy, respectively.

To understand the chart, consider the first row, which is the situation when the commodity has a realized price of $75. If the comparison reference price is $100, the price that could be locked in with the forward contract, then the manager who decided to "do nothing" would be quite happy. They will be able to purchase the commodity for the now reduced price of $75,

---

[2]Most risk managers will compare their hedge strategy to the forward price as that is the fair price at which they could have "fixed" their price if they so desired.

Possible price of underlying commodity in 3 months' time	Relative value of "do nothing" strategy	Relative value of buy forward strategy	Relative value of buy call option strategy
75	25	−25	15
80	20	−20	10
85	15	−15	5
90	10	−10	0
95	5	−5	−5
100	0	0	−10
105	−5	5	−5
110	−10	10	0
115	−15	15	5
120	−20	20	10
125	−25	25	15

Figure 2.1 *Relative value of different hedging strategies*

thus saving $25 by adopting their "do nothing" strategy. The purchaser of the forward contract will be in a different situation. While they get to buy the commodity at the fixed price of $100 (by the terms of the forward contract, they have to buy at $100), they will realize that they are at a $25 disadvantage to the current market price of $75. Thus, the purchaser of the forward contract will have a $25 opportunity loss. The purchaser of the call option now has an option that is worthless. They will not exercise their option to buy at $100, but instead will buy at the lower current market price of $75, saving $25 from the reference price of $100. However, they paid $10 for the unexercised option, and so their net relative value will be a positive $15.

The situation is somewhat reversed if the price of the commodity soars to $125 by the maturity date. In this case, the manager who chose to do nothing will buy at the higher current market price of $125 and have a $25 loss compared with the reference price of $100. The purchaser of the forward will be quite pleased as they get to purchase at the locked-in forward price of $100, and thus realize a $25 saving from the current market price. Likewise, the buyer of the call option will exercise their call option and purchase the commodity at the strike price of $100, and thus save

$25. However, the buyer of the call option paid an upfront $10 premium and so their net savings is $15.

There are a couple of key facts to note about the chart. First, you should notice that the outcomes from the do-nothing strategy mirror the outcomes from the forward strategy. If it is equally likely that the price of the commodity could go up or go down, then the expected relative value from the do-nothing strategy is the exact same as the expected relative value from the forward strategy. If the price goes down the do-nothing strategy outperforms, while if the price goes up, the forward strategy performs best. The second thing to notice is that the option strategy is always the second best strategy, and furthermore it is second best by the amount of the premium paid. For instance, if prices go down, the do-nothing strategy is best, the option strategy is second best, and the forward strategy is worst. Conversely, if prices rise, then the forward strategy is best, the option strategy is second best, while the do-nothing strategy is worst. Fundamentally, there is no strategy that performs "best" in all situations.

Hedging with forwards allows for price certainty, which in turn makes planning more straightforward. By hedging with forwards, a firm will be hedged against adverse price moves, but by locking in the cost, they will not be able to take advantage of advantageous price moves. The option strategy allows one to hedge against adverse price moves, yet still benefit from advantageous price moves. However, there is a cost for this flexibility, namely the option premium.

Case Study

Southwest Airlines

To illustrate a real-life scenario of contrasting the do-nothing strategy versus using forwards, it is useful to consider the case of Southwest Airlines and its hedging of jet fuel.

According to the IATA, the airline industry will spend US$130 billion on fuel in 2017, accounting for 17 percent of all operating expenses. To put this into perspective, total industry profits are expected to be $34.5 billion. Assuming increases in fuel costs cannot be passed on to customers, but are absorbed by the airlines, it would only take slightly more than a 25 percent increase in fuel costs to wipe out the profits of the entire industry! Given how volatile energy prices are, this seems to be a very realistic possibility. There are several financial products that can be used to hedge exposure to jet fuel, including crude oil futures that are very liquid and highly correlated to jet fuel prices, so hedging products are readily available for airlines. The question of whether or not to hedge is strategic, and several external dimensions must be considered. Can fuel cost increases be passed on to customers? We have seen many airlines implement fuel surcharges that help cover higher fuel costs, but there may be limits to how much customers are willing to absorb. Importantly, the behavior of competitors must be considered. If you choose to hedge and your competitor does not, then if fuel prices rise you are in a great position—your competitor will have increased costs that they will have to pass on to customers making their airfares more expensive or they will end up with lower profits if they don't raise prices.

Many airlines decide not to hedge, including some that have abandoned hedging programs when things seemed to be going against them, but Southwest Airlines has been a strong proponent of hedging through oil's ups and downs. In 2008, as oil prices rose to record highs, Southwest had praise heaped on its hedging program. Wired magazine published an article titled *Southwest Airlines' Seven Secrets for Success*. One of those secrets was, of course, "aggressive fuel hedging." Wired stated:

> Rampaging fuel prices now represent around 40 percent of an airline's costs, but, as usual, Southwest Airlines has been ahead of the curve. Since 1999, the airline's aggressive fuel-hedging program has saved it an estimated $3.5 billion. In the first quarter, for example, it paid $1.98 a gallon for fuel, approximately a dollar less than its network competitors. And Southwest's future position is admirable: It is 70 percent hedged at $51 a barrel through the end of the year and 55 percent hedged at the same price next year.[3]

The admirable future position didn't work out exactly as planned, as only 3 months later Southwest reported its first quarterly loss in 17 years

---

[3]J. Brancatelli. 2008. "Southwest Airlines' Seven Secrets for Success." https://www.wired.com/2008/07/southwest-airlines-seven-secrets-for-success

thanks to a $247 million charge related to the declining value of its hedging contracts. As the New York Times reported, "Southwest Airlines has long been the envy of the industry for its foresight in arranging contracts to lock in jet fuel prices. But its strategy may have backfired now that oil prices have dropped."[4] Those conflicting views of hedging are not uncommon in the media and general public—when hedges are in the money, the hedger is deemed a genius and when out of the money, the hedger is thought a fool. Of course, the truth is that if the objective of a hedging program is to mitigate exposure to market prices, a mix of gains and losses are to be expected over time as prices rise and fall. The success of a hedging program should not be measured only in hedging gains and losses, but in how much volatility has been removed from the underlying exposure.

This example illustrates the importance of understanding the competitive landscape, and clearly articulating the objectives and risks of a hedging program to all relevant stakeholders including shareholders, investment analysts, and ratings agencies.

Physical versus Cash-Settlement

Derivatives can be cash settled or physically settled. In a physically settled transaction, the actual underlying commodity is exchanged for the full dollar value specified in the contract. For example, assume a forward contract on oil with a notional amount of 5,000 barrels and a forward price of $52 per barrel. At the maturity of the contract, the forward buyer would pay $52 multiplied by 5,000 barrels and in return receive 5,000 barrels of oil. This transaction has a lot of operational components associated with it. Firstly, there is a large transfer of monies. Secondly, there is a transfer of 5,000 barrels of oil. Particularly for the financial intermediaries that frequently make a market in these transactions, these are cumbersome operational details to manage. Thus most (not all) derivative transactions are cash settled.

In a cash-settled transaction, only the cash value of the economic transaction is exchanged at maturity. Continuing with our forward example,

---

[4]M. Maynard. 2008. "Southwest Has First Loss in 17 Years," *The New York Times*. http://www.nytimes.com/2008/10/17/business/17air.html

assume at maturity that the market price of oil was $61 per barrel. In this case, the seller of the forward would deliver the difference between the market price and the contract price or $61 minus $52, or $9 per barrel to the forward buyer. Thus, the seller of the forward would pay the forward buyer $9 multiplied by 5,000 barrels, or a total of $45,000. Conversely, if the market price of oil is below the forward price, for example $48 per barrel, then the forward buyer would pay the forward seller the difference or, in this example, $20,000 ($52 minus $48 multiplied by 5,000 barrels). Note that in both cases, if the forward buyer purchases oil at the current market price, then their all-in cost including the forward payments will work out to be as if they purchased the oil for the contracted price of $52 per barrel.

Cash-settled transactions are much easier to deal with, and provide both the buyer and seller of the derivative more flexibility and thus they are more common.

Exchange Traded versus Over-the-Counter Derivatives

Forwards and options can be bought or sold directly between two counterparties, or they can be bought and sold on an exchange. Although the economics of the two methods are virtually identical in concept, there are advantages and disadvantages to each of the approaches. The mechanics also differ in two significant ways. Forward contracts that are traded on an exchange are called futures contracts, in part to distinguish them from forwards based on their operational characteristics. Economically, forwards and futures are very similar and conceptually behave in virtually identical fashion when they are used for risk management.

When trading derivatives on an exchange, the contracts are standardized. That is, the time to maturity, the notional size, the location of delivery (if it is to be physically settled), and the actual specific commodity being traded (for instance, 3-month interest rates, versus 2-month interest rates, or corn yellow number 2, versus corn yellow number 3) are all highly specified and standardized. This standardization facilitates trading, and creates more liquidity than would otherwise be available, but it makes designing a perfect hedge even more difficult than usual. It is highly unlikely that the exchange-set maturity dates, the exchange-set notional amounts, and the exchange-set specifications for the actual commodity will be exactly what are desired by a company that wishes to hedge an exposure. Exchanges set the terms and standardization of their contracts as a compromise between the needs of both speculators as well as hedgers. Designing contracts to attract speculators helps improve pricing, and it increases liquidity and ease of trading, but it does so at some compromise to the flexibility desired by the hedgers.

In an over-the-counter trade, which is a negotiated trade between two counterparties of which one is generally a financial institution, the terms of the contract can be set to whatever the two counterparties agree upon. There are few limits as to how the contract can be designed. The implicit cost for this is that the more bespoke the contract is, the less liquidity, or the fewer counterparties there will be to trade out of the contract if the risk management needs of one of the counterparties change. This lack of liquidity may also have explicit costs, as the more bespoke the contract, the more likely there will be hidden embedded fees. The advantage for the hedger is that they get a contract that exactly meets their hedging specifications.

A second difference in the mechanics is the aspect of counterparty risk. When entering into an over-the-counter derivative contract, there is the risk that your counterparty may not be able (or willing) to fulfill their contractual obligations. This is called counterparty risk. For over-the-counter trades, counterparty risk is managed by limiting the amount of counterparty exposure to any given counterparty, and by ensuring that you only trade with highly rated counterparties. This is why the counterparty in an over-the-counter trade is almost always a highly rated financial institution.

When you trade on an exchange, in effect you are trading with the exchange itself. Since all the contracts are standardized, it also implies that they are fungible. Thus, the exchange in effect creates a pool of buyers and sellers and internally matches them up through the actions of market makers. To ensure fulfillment of contracts, the exchange requires all traders (and market makers) to post margin, except in the case of buying an option, in which case the premium is paid upfront so there is no counterparty risk in respect to the option buyer (but there is counterparty risk to the option seller). This margin is adjusted on a daily basis depending on whether the contract increased or decreased in value for each counterparty. If the value of the contract increased, then that counterparty's margin account is credited, while conversely the margin account is debited for the counterparty whose side of the contract decreased in value that day. If a margin account falls below some preset threshold, then that counterparty will be required to add more cash (or equivalents) to their margin account, in what is labeled a margin call. If the counterparty is unwilling or unable to meet the demands in a timely fashion, then their account is closed out at a loss and penalties may be incurred.

The significance of margin calls is that they imply that a firm using exchange traded contracts may have to make interim cash payments in order to satisfy a margin call. In Chapter 7, a case study of the German conglomerate Metallgesellschaft will be discussed. Metallgesellschaft was using short-term futures contracts to hedge a very large, and a very long-term oil price risk. Due to fluctuations in oil prices, the company faced a very large series of margin calls amounting to over \$1.3 billion. Many experts believe that the company would have more than recouped these cash flows at the expiration of their long-term oil deals, but the interim cash flows required by the exchanges forced it to close out its risk management strategy at a huge loss. The case of Metallgesellschaft is a cautionary tale about margin calls, albeit a very extreme case.

A major advantage of exchange traded derivatives is the price transparency. The exchanges publish continuously updated prices, so when a trade is made, a company has a relatively high degree of confidence that the price is a fair one.[5] As risk management needs are likely to change, it means that companies will need to change their hedges and thus enter into new contracts and perhaps settle early, or close out, some existing contracts. In such cases, having price transparency, along with the extra liquidity of an exchange traded derivative can be a significant advantage.

Closing or Canceling a Trade

In reality, almost all exchange traded derivative contracts are closed, or canceled, before expiration. This is especially true for commodity

---

[5]Note that if a price on an exchange is out of line, or unfair, market speculators and arbitragers will immediately step in and take advantage of the mispricing until the price moves back to a fair level.

contracts that are physically settled. This is in large part due to the standardization of exchange traded contracts not matching the exact needs of the hedger. The contract in essence gets settled for its fair market value, and then a new series of contracts may be entered into. As most exchange traded derivatives have relatively short terms to maturity, it is often necessary for companies to enter into a series of contracts one after another. This is another reason why such a large proportion of exchange traded contracts are closed out early. Over-the-counter trades may also be closed out early if the risk management needs of the company have changed and contracts with different terms are now needed.

To close out an exchange traded contract, it is normal practice to enter into an equivalent contract, but in the opposite direction. For example, if one bought a futures contract for expiry in May, then one would close out that trade by selling an equivalent number of the same contract that also expire in May. The exchange then internally cancels the buy side and the sell side of the transaction.

Since the price of the underlying of the derivative contract would have likely changed in price since the inception of the original trade, this also implies that the value of the contract would have changed. Thus, the net proceeds received from closing out a derivatives contract early is the change in value of the contract—which could of course be positive or negative. The value of a contract at any time is called the mark-to-market value. That is, it is the price of the contract based on the market values of the pricing variables that go into pricing the contract.

The pricing of contracts is beyond the scope of this book. There are several websites and data providers that provide pricing calculators, and of course the price of a contract is always visible for exchange traded derivatives.[6]

For over-the-counter trades, the price to close out the transaction will be negotiated between the counterparties. The counterparties will agree to cancel the trade for a negotiated fair value. This is where the hedger may be at the mercy of the counterparty if they do not have access to pricing software or pricing screens. In such cases, it is always best to shop various

---

[6]Readers interested in the pricing of derivatives can consult a textbook such as J. HulJ. 2017. *Options, Futures and Other Derivatives* (10th ed., Boston, MA: Pearson).

dealers to get their respective prices on the transaction. It may be better value to do the offsetting trade with another dealer. This of course would not cancel the trade, and the hedger would in fact have two outstanding trades, but economically they would cancel each other out. The only residual exposure would be the counterparty risk to not just one, but now two counterparties.

Swaps

Swaps are in essence a series of forward contracts that settle on a set of periodic dates. In a typical swap, one counterparty agrees to make a payment based on a notional amount and the market price of an index or a commodity, and the other counterparty agrees to make a fixed payment based on the same notional amount.

One of the most common examples of a swap is an interest rate swap. Figure 2.2 illustrates this.

In this example swap, the two counterparties have an agreement where every 6 months for a period of 5 years, they will exchange payments. The swap will be based on a notional amount—for instance $10 million. The fixed rate payer will then pay the notional amount, multiplied by the fixed swap rate, multiplied by the day count ratio since the last payment. If the swap payments are made every 6 months, then the day count ratio would be one-half, since it was half a year since the previous payment.[7] The floating rate payer also makes a payment which in this example is based on the

Figure 2.2 Illustration of an interest rate swap

Dashed line shows floating rate payments, while solid line illustrates fixed rate payments.

---

[7]There are a variety of different ways of calculating the day count ratio. The specifics of the day count ratio are specified in the swap contract. For an interest rate swap, the day count ratio is generally set up so it matches the day count ratio on a loan that it is hedging.

LIBOR, the London Interbank Offer Rate, which is a floating rate index that is frequently used as the basis for floating rate loans. The payment by the floating rate payer will be the notional amount, multiplied by the LIBOR setting for the period in question, and again multiplied by the day count ratio. Generally, only the net payment is made. If the LIBOR for the period is higher than the fixed rate, then the floating rate payer will make a net payment of the difference to the fixed rate payer. Conversely, if the fixed rate is greater than the LIBOR for the period, then the fixed rate payer will make a net payment to the floating rate payer. It is effectively the same as if the two counterparties had entered into 10 separate forward contracts, based on the LIBOR interest rate and with each forward price set at the fixed rate agreed to in the swap.

Swaps can be based on interest rates, commodity prices, exchange rates, energy prices, and even equity prices. Figure 2.3 illustrates an example of a commodity swap based on oil prices.

In Figure 2.3, assume that it is a 3-year, quarterly swap, based on a notional amount of 5,000 barrels of oil. Also assume that the fixed oil price (the swap rate) is $52 per barrel. Thus, in this example, every 3 months, the fixed rate payer will make a payment of $52 multiplied by 5,000 barrels to the floating rate payer, and in return the floating rate payer will make a payment of 5,000 barrels multiplied by what the market price of oil was for that period. Again, the payments are generally netted, so if the market price is above $52, then the floating rate payer will make a net payment, and conversely if the market price for the period is below $52, then the fixed rate payer will make a net payment. In effect, this swap is equivalent to the fixed rate payer entering into 12 different forward contracts spread out with maturity dates over the next 3 years, to buy 500 barrels of oil at a forward price of $52 per barrel.

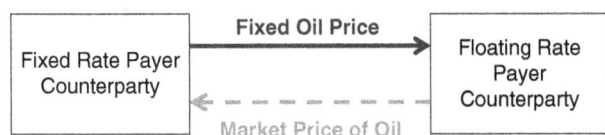

Figure 2.3 Illustration of a commodity swap

Dashed line shows floating rate payments and solid line shows fixed payments.

Swaps are a very convenient tool for hedging a series of financial risk exposures such as the interest payments on a loan, a regular purchase of a commodity, regular transfers of foreign currency, and a variety of other regularly occurring transactions. Given their flexibility, swaps are the workhorse of financial risk management.

Concluding Thoughts

To briefly summarize, there are two main classes of financial risk management strategies; operational strategies and the use of financial derivatives. Operational strategies should form the backbone of long-term and ongoing financial risk exposures. However, operational strategies tend to create long-term commitments, such as building a foreign plant, and tend to be blunt instruments if used solely for financial risk management purposes. Thus, the use of derivatives acts as a nice complement to operational strategies, as derivatives can be used as a flexible tool to fine-tune the risk management strategy to account for risks that are more transactional in nature.

CHAPTER 3

Financial Risk Management Frameworks

Introduction

A risk management framework is where a corporation generally begins its implementation of a formalized risk management strategy. There are a variety of pros and cons to have a financial risk management framework. Likewise, there are a wide variety of suggested frameworks available, and in this chapter we will also put forward our suggested framework. However, we believe it is only common sense that a framework should be developed by the managers of an organization to fit the specific risk management needs and objectives of their organization. As such, each risk management framework should be unique to the organization, rather than a cookie-cutter one-size-fits-all that is promoted by one organization or another.

Before putting forth what we believe are the essential elements in a financial risk management framework, it is useful to briefly discuss some of the pros and cons of risk frameworks in general. An understanding of the advantages and disadvantages is helpful as an organization considers what elements should be in their framework.

The major knock against risk frameworks is that they tend to become an entity onto themselves. That is, they become too large, too intricate, and too bureaucratic to be efficient tools for directing the risk management process.

A bloated risk framework has the potential to do much more harm than good. A bloated risk framework tends to "crowd out" risk thinking as managers start managing for the risk framework rather than managing for good risk management. In other words, the risk framework becomes the management objective rather than good risk management. This in turn leads to a shift in accountability away from the manager to the framework. How often have you heard that "all guidelines were followed" as an excuse for a risk miscue, when it was obvious that while the risk guidelines were followed, common sense was not. It is never a positive when managers can abdicate their responsibility and accountability for thinking, analysis, and making good decisions and instead simply default to a framework or a process. Strong frameworks and processes do have value—which we will discuss shortly—but they are very poor replacements for judgment.

A related effect is risk homeostasis, which is the effect that increasing the strength and power of your risk frameworks and processes actually, and paradoxically, has a tendency to lead to an overall increased level of risk. If it is believed that a strong risk framework is in place, the natural response of people is to change their risk taking behavior. Consider how different your driving habits would be if you were driving in a winter snow blizzard in a modern SUV with the latest in traction control and upgraded snow tires, versus how you would drive in the same snowstorm in an older model econobox with bald summer tires and without the benefit of electronic traction control. In all likelihood you would reconsider the necessity of making a journey in the blizzard if you only had the econobox car at your disposal. This is why we see that the probability of being injured is actually greater when driving an SUV versus an econobox car. This is the effect of risk homeostasis and it is one unintended consequence of having too strong a risk management framework.[1]

An extensive risk framework is also costly. It entails both explicit costs as well as hidden implicit costs. The explicit costs include management's time, energy, and effort to set up and implement. Additionally, depending on the extensiveness of the system, there may be significant information technology and data feeds requirements. An overly costly framework may involve hiring full-time risk specialists. All of these costs will pay dividends only if the risk management requirements of the firm justify the expense.

---

[1]For more on risk homeostasis, see R. Nason. October, 2009. "Is Your Risk System Too Good?," *RMA Journal*. Also see R. Nason. 2017. "Is Your Risk Management Too Good?" In *Experts Insight Collection*. New York, NY: Business Experts Press.

The implicit costs of too extensive a risk management framework include having the system actually preventing new ideas from coming to the fore due to the perceived hassle of meeting the requirements of the risk management system. It may also encourage managers from seeking out the assistance of the risk management department if it is seen as a bureaucratic nightmare. An overbearing and bureaucratic risk framework could even discourage managers from expanding into profitable new markets or product segments.

Most ominously, an overly cumbersome risk management system may incent managers to find ways to circumvent the system entirely—which can be the most costly consequence of all. In many of the risk management workshops that we have conducted, the risk management department is frequently seen as the "Department of No!" This is obviously not what the desired reputation of a value-added department should be. If the culture around the risk framework is negative, then the culture around risk management activities will also be negative. Risk management should be seen as a positive that is allowing managers to more effectively do their central task of producing and marketing goods and services. A lean and simple risk management framework helps risk management be viewed as an asset for the manager, while an overbearing, cumbersome, and time consuming risk framework will make risk management an adversary to the line manager.

Obviously, not all of the consequences of a risk framework are negative. After all, we are recommending that an organization develop their own risk management framework before starting a financial risk management program. The major advantage of a risk management framework is that it provides a common structure around which a common shared understanding of risk management can be built and expanded upon as needed. This common thread brings economies of scale to the risk management process and helps the organization develop institutional experience and learning about the best risk management strategies and tactics for reaching its objectives.

A suitably comprehensive risk framework prevents an ad-hoc series of risk management solutions arising throughout the firm. Starting with a framework allows for a coordinated and consistent process that will capture risk management synergies and efficiencies. Frequently, when risk management is done on an ad-hoc or even on an as-needed basis, there is more room for errors and mistakes to creep into the process. Additionally, ad-hoc risk management implementations tend to be redundant or even self-defeating due to the fact that it is difficult to track the overall level of risk and the overall level of risk management strategies in place without a central framework to coordinate the information.

A risk management framework also provides a checklist to help ensure that all of the necessary steps and processes have been followed or at a minimum considered. A good risk management framework allows the manager to have the confidence that a framework is ensuring that care of the routine tasks of risk management is taking place while the manager can focus their energies on considering the specifics of each risk management situation. Having a framework act as a checklist that ensures that the necessary steps have been considered is a simple, yet very effective aid to efficient risk management.[2]

Essentials of a Good Framework

A good risk framework has some very basic, intuitive, and simple elements. To begin, a good risk framework is one that is lean and simple. Lean and simple encourage adherence to the framework, and adherence to a framework, even if it is potentially missing some bells and whistles, is still far better than ignoring, or avoiding the most comprehensive yet unwieldy of frameworks. The framework should be practical and easy to ensure implementation for the various situations that the firm may face.

A good risk framework is also flexible and adaptable to the wide variety of financial risks that the firm may encounter. The system should be expandable to encompass future needs, and for that matter it should also be contractible if the needs of the organization for risk management decrease.

Critically, the risk framework should be tied to the risk management objectives of the firm. If the risk management framework is not in synch with the risk management objectives of the organization, then little else matters. Ultimately, this requirement means that the risk framework

---

[2]For more on the value of using checklists see, A. Gawande. 2009. *The Checklist Manifesto: How To Get Things Right* (New York, NY: Henry Holt and Company).

should be tailored to the firm. Off-the-shelf systems recommended by consultants are likely to be too broad, and too generic to suit the needs of the firm, and are also quite likely to have extraneous features that simply add to the cost and confusion of its use while adding little of positive value.

Despite the fact that a good risk framework should be lean, simple, flexible, and tailored to the organization, there are certain key elements that should be present in almost every financial risk management framework. These elements are listed here.

A Clear Objective for the Risk Management Function

Without a clear objective, it is nearly impossible to have effective risk management. This should be the first task in developing a risk management program and a task that is periodically revisited to ensure that it remains timely and appropriate.

While there are many excellent reasons to implement a financial risk management program, there needs to be a strategic objective if one hopes to do so in an effective and consistent manner. Many risk management objectives can be at odds with each other, and thus without a clear objective there are likely to be conflicts and inefficiencies. For instance, is the goal of the financial risk management program to eliminate financial risk? That is one possible risk management objective, but if so, it ignores the situations when an organization may want to take advantage of financial risk. (Remember, risk is the possibility that bad or good things may happen and there are a range of possible responses to risk.) As discussed in Chapter 2, there are a variety of risk management tools which permit an organization to choose different risk management objectives. These objectives need to be clarified at the very beginning.

The risk management objectives should be carefully thought through by management and approved by the Board. Risk management can be a major component of a company's competitive strategy and as such it should be treated with the same amount of respect and thoughtful analysis as any other strategic or competitive decision.

We will devote more discussion to the setting of the financial risk management strategy in Chapter 10.

Identify Risks

The identification of risks, both existing risks as well as potential risks, is an obvious and necessary component of any decent risk framework. You cannot manage what you cannot identify. It also relates to what we call the first law of risk management; the mere fact that you acknowledge that a risk exists automatically increases the probability and magnitude of it occurring if it is a good risk while also automatically decreasing the probability and severity of it occurring if it is a bad risk. Perhaps it is easier stated to say that merely being aware of the risks means the risk management battle is half won.

The process of identifying the risks is also key in that it forces the organization to be more aware of how financial risks affect the firm's performance. Actively working to identify risks forces managers to think about how their organization works and the relationship of the various financial risks and the various linkages with the operations of the firm.

When identifying risks, it is critical to consider not only the existing risks, but also potential risks. A key element of risk is that it is a forward-looking activity. However, too often risk management systems are backward looking, collecting data on things that did happen, or are happening in the present, rather than focusing on what might happen going forward. Managers can only affect the future, and are helpless about changing the past. That is not to say that the past should be ignored. Understanding what happened in the past from a risk management standpoint aids in learning valuable lessons that can be applied in improving future risk management strategies and tactics.

Additionally, it is important to identify the strategic financial risks. It is generally relatively easy to identify and measure the financial risks based on transactions (such as foreign sales transactions, or interest rate risk due to financing obligations), but it is a more subtle, but perhaps more important task to identify the hidden and less overt strategic financial risks. Examples of strategic risk are the effects that exchange rates could have on a company's competitive position relative to its foreign-based peers, or the effect that a change in commodity prices could have on a firm's supply chain and pricing strategies.

Measure Risks

When managers think of managing financial risk, the step of measuring the risks is generally considered to be the most quantitative and the one requiring the most specialist mathematical knowledge. While it is indeed the fact that advances in the measurement of financial risks has developed some highly sophisticated mathematical techniques, the reality is that even simple measures of quantifying the size of the risks goes a long way in helping to manage those risks.

As management guru Peter Drucker is alleged to have said, "what gets measured, gets managed" is certainly true for risk management. Conversely, it is also generally, but not always, true that what does not get measured does not get managed. However, in recent years, there has been an overreliance on the measurement and not enough energy spent on the management of the risk. The goal of risk management should be the management of risk, not just the measurement of risk. While we agree that being aware of the risks is half the battle of risk management, it is most certainly not sufficient. Regulators in particular seem to have an obsession on risk measurement and mistakenly conflate measurement with risk management.

Choose and Implement Risk Action

The decision phase of how to best manage the risks is obviously the centerpiece of any risk management process. Recalling the definition of risk (the possibility that bad or good things may happen), it is important when making a choice on managing risks to consider the full range of risk responses. Recalling from Chapter 2, the full range of risk responses are: (i) Avoid or Eliminate, (ii) Mitigate, (iii) Tolerate but Monitor, (iv) Ignore, (v) Embellish, and (vi) Embrace. The choice of risk response will determine the type and style of the risk management technique or tool chosen. Too often, firms just automatically assume that risks should be avoided or eliminated, and enter into a costly and counterproductive risk management strategy. We have also seen companies adopt two or even three different risk management strategies as they could not make a choice as to which of the risk responses was appropriate! For example, one firm we dealt with, simultaneously used three different tactics when dealing with currency risk. Being unsure how to hedge, they would leave one-third of the risk unhedged, would hedge another third with forwards, and would use option strategies for hedging the third portion of the exposure. It was the equivalent of not being able to make up your mind when ordering ice-cream, and thus getting a mixture of every flavor. An expensive and totally ineffective way to manage risk.

If the firm has a clear risk management objective, the choice of the risk response should be relatively straightforward. If the firm does not have a well-defined and well-delineated financial risk management objective, then the risk response decision is likely to be muddled at best.

After the risk response has been chosen, the tool or tactic(s) for managing the risk should be chosen. This includes whether it will be an operational strategy or something like insurance, selling off the risk, or a derivative management tool. The choice of tactic or tool will also have a series of choices that follow. For instance, if a derivative management strategy is chosen, the firm needs to choose what type of derivative, whether it will be an over-the-counter derivative, or an exchange traded derivative, the terms of the derivative (such as notional amount, strike price, or tenor), and who the counterparty for the derivative will be.

The choice of risk action thus involves both strategic as well as operational decisions. A risk management tactic that ignores this reality is likely to be ineffective at best and counterproductive at worst.

Monitor and Assess Risk Management Effectiveness

Most companies with a financial risk management program do monitor their risk management, but in our experience few can tell whether or not their risk management actions are being effective and helping to forward both the risk management objective as well as the strategic objective of the firm. As with measurement, risk monitoring is often done in large part as a regulatory exercise, not as the business improvement function that it should be.

There are two parts to this step of the risk management process. One is to monitor the risk management function. This would be aspects such as what are the cost and the value of the hedges, what is the concentrations of the counterparties to the hedges, what are the size and timing of any cash flows related to the hedges, when do the hedges expire or need to be renewed or updated, what is the overall level of hedges relative to the exposure, as well as other possible related metrics that need to be continuously checked and monitored. The second part of this step is to assess whether the hedges are performing the function that they were put in place to accomplish. Are the hedges helping to manage the risk and achieve the operational and strategic objectives of the firm?

Monitoring and assessing the risk management function implies taking a look back at what transpired and how well the risk management strategy worked relative to other alternatives. It is also ensuring that the tactics used achieved the objectives set out. Note, it is not an exercise in deciding whether the particular strategy chosen was optimal given the economic events that followed. It is deciding if the strategy chosen was optimal given what was known at the time that the risk management strategy was chosen. Hindsight is wonderful, but making judgments based on hindsight is impractical and misleading.

Effective Reporting and Communication

The risk management process should not be the purview of a select few. It should be a transparent process that is widely communicated and widely understood. Effective communication of the risk management strategy and outcomes has many benefits. Effective risk reporting helps with organizational learning about risk, engagement with risk, and is a key component of developing a positive risk culture.

A good risk report shows a timely indicator of the existing risks as well as expected risks. It also gives a clear indication of what risk management efforts are implemented and how effective they are. It also aids in making future decisions about risk management strategies.

The centerpiece of a risk report should be a risk dashboard. Risk dashboards will be discussed at more length in Chapter 10, but now it suffices to realize that a risk dashboard gives the key risk indicators for the firm. Just like a car's dashboard, a risk dashboard gives only those key indicators that the management team needs to achieve their objectives, as well as warning signals (such as the check engine light) that point to the need for a more detailed look at an issue. While extensive risk reports are a tool for the risk professional, a slimmed-down risk dashboard report is likely to be a more effective tool for the general manager. Some companies spend so much time preparing comprehensive and detailed risk reports that they are well out of date by the time they can be read and understood by managers.

Other Considerations

Other important elements of a good risk management framework are: appropriate training, appropriate accountability, and integration with the enterprise risk management system—if the organization practices enterprise risk management.

Appropriate training is required not only for frontline managers, but also for the senior management team and especially for the Board. In order to ensure a consistent approach to risk management, and to ensure that the risk management tactics are in line with the strategic objective set by the Board, operational managers, senior managers, and the Board need training that ensures all are consistent in their understanding of the risk management process, how to implement and assess the various elements, and how to communicate about risk effectively.

Although implementation of the financial risk management process may be accomplished through a dedicated risk management department which is appropriately staffed by risk management specialists, risk management is not a task that should only be understood by those experts. Leaving the risk management solely to a dedicated department means that opportunities for enhanced risk management will be almost certainly missed. A well-trained staff can alert the risk management function to opportunities, and by understanding what risk management can, and cannot accomplish, there will be better communication between the line and risk management. This enhanced communication in turn means greater acceptance of risk management, broader accountability for risk management, and that risk management will reciprocally be brought in earlier as operational plans are being formulated, thus allowing for risk management to be more fully integrated into the strategic planning process.

The Board and senior managers need extensive risk training so they too can better implement risk management into operations and the strategic planning process. Additionally, the Board needs a full appreciation of risk management so they can practice better risk governance, by asking better questions, getting better responses, and having better overall discussions of how risk management can improve the operations of the firm.

For the risk process, clear lines of accountability need to be set up. Although in a perfect world, everyone would be accountable for risk management, the reality is that it is not practical to do so. Clear lines for accountability in terms of who is ultimately responsible for the risk strategy, who is responsible for implementing risk tactics, and who is responsible for verifying the checks and balances needed to ensure compliance with the strategy and set tolerance levels are needed. In part, extensive training and appropriate risk communication systems will play a large role in setting up the appropriate checks and balances. However, without oversight and accountability, flaws will still be likely to go through the system unchecked without a specific oversight function. In large part, financial risk management has achieved its reputation as being too tricky or too fraught with potential for mistakes or fraud due in large part to an absence of appropriate oversight or accountability. The oversight does not have to be stifling; it just needs to be in place with clear accountability.

Finally, the risk management process should fit with the enterprise risk management system and processes of the organization. Not all organizations, particularly smaller organizations, have a full enterprise risk management system. However, for those that do, the financial risk management system should integrate seamlessly with it. This does not mean that the financial risk management system needs to be the same as the enterprise risk management system (in general they should be different), but they should integrate and be consistent and have compatible measurement and reporting systems, and consistent terminology.

With the increase in the importance of data analytics, and the increasing awareness of how risk management, both financial risk management and enterprise risk management, can so greatly help an organization achieve its objectives and gain competitive advantage, it is likely that the number of organizations implementing enterprise risk management systems will grow significantly in the future.[3]

The elements of our suggested risk management framework essentials are summarized in Figure 3.1.

---

[3]For a guide to Enterprise Risk Management, see the companion book of R. Nason and L. Fleming. 2018. *Essentials of Enterprise Risk Management* (New York, NY: Business Experts Press).

Figure 3.1 Risk management framework essentials

The Financial Risk Questions

Before concluding this chapter, it is instructive to look at a series of questions that should be asked about any financial risk management decision. These six questions can act as a guide to making financial risk management decisions. Of course, this list is not exhaustive, and each organization should think about what questions would be appropriate to add to deal with their own specific situations.

The first three questions to ask about a financial risk are: what can happen, when can it happen, and how much of an effect can it have? These questions form the fundamentals of the terms of the hedge instrument.

The next question to ask is how does the risk fit with the strategic objective? Does the risk have more potential to be a good risk or a bad risk? Is it a risk that is key for the strategic objective to be achieved? Is it a risk that can lead to competitive advantage or disadvantage? Does the risk provide some sort of tactical advantage or disadvantage? Is it a risk that is key to this firm, or is it a risk that other competitors need to deal with as well? Good financial risk management is always considering the ultimate objective. Risk management is to work solely for the good of the organization; not necessarily for the good of the risk management function.

When considering the strategic component of risk management, it is important to realize that stakeholders may have a different objective; in particular, financial stakeholders may be investing in the company solely because they want the company to embrace financial risks. For instance, many equity investors in gold mining companies are doing so specifically because they want the commodity risk exposure to gold prices. However, if the gold mining company has completely hedged their gold price exposure, investors will not be achieving the exposure that they invested for in. In part, this is another reason why an organization needs to be very clear in what the financial risk management objective is, and in being completely transparent in communicating that risk management objective.

Finally, in developing the risk management process, an organization has to take account of its capabilities in terms of financial risk management. Does it have the knowledge and understanding of the various risks and risk management instruments that it is trying to use? Does it have the systems and data analysis capabilities to appropriately manage their risk management positions? Can it measure with reasonable accuracy its hedge exposures? Does it have appropriate measures in place to account for and measure counterparty exposure? Often, organizations develop risk management tactics that are beyond their capability to implement and adequately monitor. The most famous example might be Procter and Gamble and the series of exotic swaps that they entered into in the mid-1990s to manage their interest rate exposure. Procter and Gamble were at the mercy of their financial counterpart Banker's Trust in terms of assessing the value of their positions and how they should revise their positions to achieve their risk management objectives. The result was a financial debacle for Procter and Gamble, and in part led to the downfall of Banker's Trust as a leading provider of risk management solutions.

Although sophisticated risk management techniques have their place, organizations should not get ahead of their capabilities. As a general rule, if a manager cannot explain what they are doing so other nonspecialist managers, and in particular Board members can understand both the advantages as well as the disadvantages of the proposed risk management technique, then that risk management technique should probably not be undertaken. Virtually all risk management debacles that have been so well documented, including the failings of Procter and Gamble, were almost always a direct result of the organization not having the proper level of understanding and the proper systems to implement such a strategy, and furthermore not having the self-esteem of their manager's to admit to such. We will discuss much more about this in Chapter 10.

Concluding Thoughts

Risk frameworks have a variety of pros and cons. Generally speaking, the advantages of starting risk management with the aid of a risk management framework outweigh the negatives. However, many organizations develop too elaborate and too cumbersome a risk management framework. The result is a bureaucratic white elephant that instead of being a catalyst for risk management becomes a drag. Risk frameworks should be lean, flexible, and designed to help the organization achieve its risk management objectives in as efficient a manner as possible.

CHAPTER 4

Financial Risk Management Metrics

Introduction

As stressed in Chapter 3, one of the essential elements of a financial risk management framework is the measurement of the risks of an organization; measurement of both the existing risks as well as the potential risks going forward. The measurement of risks is obviously one of the most quantitative aspects of risk management. As such, it has the reputation of being the one task of risk management that is best left to the specialists; the quantitative analysts, more commonly called the "quants." We do not agree with that sentiment. Although the details of the calculations are beyond the scope and intentions of this book, the essentials of financial risk metrics are easily learned, and need to be learned by everyone connected with financial risk management.

In this chapter, we are going to introduce the major financial risk management metrics and explain both how they are used and misused. We are not going to go into the details of the calculations. Many of the calculations are already embedded in risk management software, and even generic spreadsheet programs like Microsoft Excel can calculate most of them almost automatically. Our aim in this chapter is to familiarize the generalist so they can conduct a useful conversation around risk—which by itself necessitates a working knowledge of risk metrics.

Before looking at specific metrics, it is important here to mention a theme that arises at several places in this book, and in this chapter. This theme is that risk management, and financial risk management in particular, is as much of an art as it is a science. Financial risk management concerns itself with a lot of variables that we can easily fool ourselves into thinking that we can measure with unlimited accuracy and precision. For instance, we talk about interest rate changes, the volatility of stock prices, and the range of gold prices, and so on. The reality is that just because we can put a number on something does not mean that we necessarily understand that variable, or that the variable will remain constant, or perhaps most importantly, that the variable we took the time to measure is even an important variable. Often, we get so excited when we can measure something that we forget to ask if it is worth measuring.

In our own educations, we were told to never start a calculation until you have an idea of what the answer should be. This is very valuable advice for risk managers. The risk calculations can become very complicated. Thus, there is the chance that we become enamored with the calculation while forgetting what the objective was. Not using intuition to develop an idea of what the answer should be before starting a formal measurement and calculation also sets the stage for a higher probability of mistakes in the calculation. If the calculation answer or measurement is far from the answer developed through intuition, then we have reason to check both our calculated answer as well as our intuition. In either case, we will find a mistake in our measurement/calculation or our intuition. At best, we correct a calculation mistake, or we develop our intuition a bit more; both good outcomes. If we have no intuitive idea of what the result of a measurement or calculation should be, then we will have no basis for judging if the answer is valid or not.

In our real-life experience, we have been in numerous situations where an experienced manager has given an intuitive answer that differed greatly from the calculated answer produced by a highly trained "quant." Almost always, the experienced manager was correct and the quant had either a mistake in calculation or a mistake in understanding the workings of the market. We believe that there is a valuable lesson in what we have observed in our own experience.

Historical Relationships

The best place to start with an assessment of risk is by measuring how risk variables and relationships performed in the past. While this is a good starting place, it is just that, a starting place. Risk is dynamic and risk relationships change. Later in this chapter, we will talk about model risk, which in part is caused by assuming that historical relationships will hold going forward. Model risk was one of the key causes of the 2008 financial crisis; quantitative risk analysts assumed that historical default relationships would continue to hold. Those default relationships did not stay constant and valuations that were considered impossible not only became possible but were smashed in reality. The point that must not be forgotten is that economic relationships are notoriously unstable.

The place to start with risk metrics is with correlations. Correlation is simply how closely two variables tend to move together. Variables that tend to move together upwards or downwards are positively correlated, while variables that tend to move in opposite directions are negatively correlated. For instance, stock prices, particularly stocks of companies in the same industry, tend to move together. Bond prices are negatively correlated with interest rates; as interest rates increase, bond prices tend to fall. Correlation values range from plus one to negative one. Two things that are perfectly correlated, so that they move in perfect lockstep, have a correlation of plus one. Likewise, variables that move perfectly opposite to each other so that when one variable is increasing the other is decreasing will have a correlation of negative one. Variables whose changes in value have no relation to each other have a correlation of zero. With real economic variables, there are no two variables that will have a perfect correlation of either a plus one or a negative one.

Correlation is important in risk management for several reasons. Correlations give a measure of sensitivity. For instance, one key risk variable is the sensitivity of sales to an economic variable such as interest rates. The elasticity of sales to interest rates (or other variables such as GDP growth) is a key part of financial risk analysis and a basic use of correlation analysis. Furthermore, costs of goods sold may be correlated to commodity prices or rates of wage inflation. Knowledge of these correlations or sensitivities and the size of these sensitivities help to both prioritize risks from most to least important and to begin the formulation of a risk management plan.

A second reason correlation is important as it helps to decide what to use as hedging instruments. If a firm is trying to eliminate a financial risk by hedging, then they want the hedging instrument they are using to have a high correlation with the variable they are concerned about. For instance, airlines need to hedge jet fuel costs (see case study on Southwest Airlines in Chapter 2). To hedge jet fuel, airlines will often enter into forward or option contracts on oil, since oil prices are highly correlated with jet fuel prices. To the extent that the correlation between the variable the firm is trying to hedge does not have a perfect correlation with the hedge instrument, there is said to be basis risk. The bigger the basis risk, the greater the chance that the hedge will not perform as desired. (Basis risk will be covered in more detail in Chapter 9 on Commodity Risk.)

Since interest rates are such an important financial risk variable, a special type of correlation is calculated called a DV01. To determine interest rate sensitivity, firms need to calculate the change in the value of their debt portfolio. This is usually done by calculating the change in value for a one basis point change in the interest rate, or the yield curve. This change in value for a theoretical one basis point change in interest rates is commonly known as "Dollar Value of a Basis Point," also known as "DV01." It is also sometimes called the "Present Value of a Basis Point," or "PV01." Many firms will also calculate a DV01 for a one basis point change in an exchange rate as a measure of their currency risk.

Calculation of correlations, or even the DV01, gives a firm a sense of how sensitive various parts of their operations are to changes in different economic variables. These correlations are a starting place for prioritizing the portfolio of risks that the firm faces. There are a couple of caveats to remember when using correlations. To begin, correlations may only hold over a small range or normal variable measures. For instance, at the time of this writing, interest rates have been abnormally low over the last decade since the 2008 financial crisis. Many traditional correlations have significantly changed and current calculations of correlation are unlikely to hold if interest rates increase to more traditional levels. Correlations are also a poor guide when extreme changes in conditions are experienced. This is especially true for DV01 calculations which are designed to measure the variable relationship for a small change in the economic variable (that is for one basis point changes). Finally, correlations tend to change during a crisis. An old adage is that all economic correlations go to one when a crisis hits, or in other words, everything tends to go down in lock-step when a crisis occurs.

Correlations are good for measuring how a variable such as sales is related to changes in one economic variable. Regression analysis is used when there might be more than one variable affecting the variables and when a measure is needed of the size of the effect. Regression analysis is simply a technique to relate the sensitivity of a variable, such as sales, to a number of different factors, such as interest rates, GDP growth, employment levels, and average earned income, simultaneously. Instead of calculating the correlations individually, a regression equation creates a formula relating the various factors to the variable in question. If one has a prediction for each of the factors in the regression equation, for instance, if one has a projection for interest rates, GDP growth, employment levels, and earned income, then one can use the results of a regression analysis to project an estimate for what sales might be.

One special regression equation for companies that have publicly traded equity is to regress the return of the company's stock returns versus interest rates and the return of the market index. The coefficient of regression for the return of the stock versus the return of the market index gives an indication of the market's perception of the overall riskiness of a company relative to other publicly traded stocks. This value is called beta. A stock with average riskiness will have a beta close to one, while a riskier-than-average stock will have a beta greater than one. Likewise, a lower-than-average-risk stock will have a beta less than one. Although there are several valid criticisms of the beta measure, the reality is that it is used by a significant number of analysts and investors to gauge the overall riskiness of a firm.

The riskiness of a variable is frequently measured by its standard deviation. Standard deviation is a measure of how much a variable moves around its historical average. The bigger the variation, the more risky the variable is. Standard deviation is generally based in the theory of the normal distribution; the normal bell-shaped curve. Figure 4.1 shows two variables that are normally distributed. While both of our hypothetical variables have the same expected value, the solid curve demonstrates more dispersion, or has the fatter distribution. Thus, the solid curve has the higher standard deviation and would be considered the higher risk variable.

Standard deviation is a useful variable if the variable in question is normally distributed, that is, it has the frequency of outcomes that

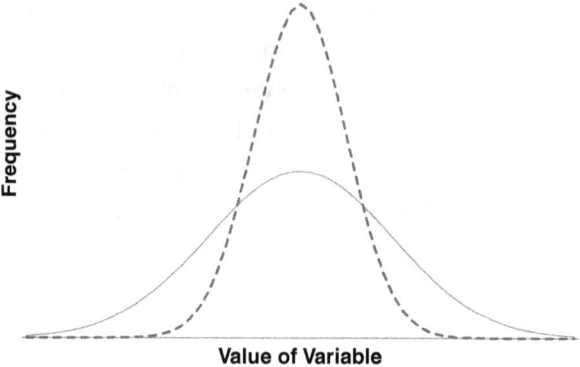

Figure 4.1 Table showing distribution of two hypothetical economic variables

The variable represented by the solid line has the higher standard deviation.

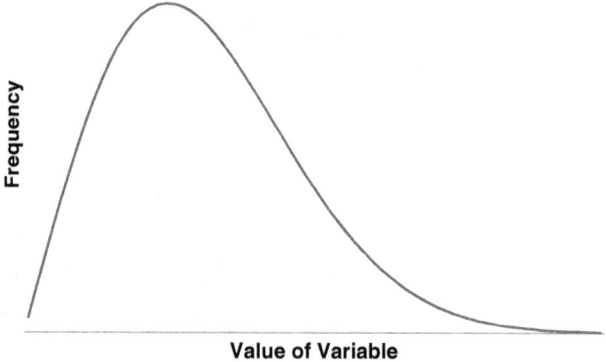

Figure 4.2 Variable with positive skew

approximate the bell-shaped curve represented in Figure 4.1. The normal distribution is symmetric in that results that are above average occur with the same frequency as the results that are below average. However, standard deviation is a poor measure of risk if the distribution is skewed, which is the case as shown in Figure 4.2. Figure 4.2 shows the frequencies of outcomes of a variable with positive skew. A variable with negative skew would have the long tail going toward negative values.

Examining the skew of a distribution is important as skew indicates whether there is more upside or downside potential. Standard deviation assumes that the distribution is symmetric, while skew gives an indication of a bias to the upside or the downside.

Another measure of risk that explicitly takes into account the upside-versus-downside variation is a measure known as semi-standard deviation. Instead of just calculating a measure of the deviations from the mean, like standard deviation does, semi-standard deviation separately calculates the level of the upside deviations separate from the level deviations on the downside. Semi-standard deviation thus allows a ratio of the upside risk to the downside risk to be calculated.

Standard deviation and the more advanced semi-standard deviation are powerful metrics that provide a picture to the variability of various economic variables. They are thus another component to rank and prioritize risks.

Monte Carlo Simulation

Once the various sensitivities between the firm's variables, and the correlations and regression factors to external financial or economic variables have been calculated, along with a measurement of how much each of the economic variables has varied in the past, then a series of forecasting techniques can be used to project how the firm might behave going forward.

One method to do so is scenario analysis. A scenario analysis is frequently done as part of the conventional economic plan. However, scenario analysis is also very useful for planning risk management strategies, and for assessing the potential outcomes of implementing such risk management strategies. The value in scenario analysis is not that any of the developed scenarios will ever occur—the probability of that happening even approximately is extremely low—but in developing intuition of how the variables affecting the firm are interrelated. In the classic reference for scenario analysis written by Peter Schwartz, he claims that good scenario analysis should be like a story[1]. For risk management purposes, scenario analysis should go beyond and be like a very creative story, as risk management needs to be able to handle the extreme unexpected outcomes.

Many corporations limit themselves to developing scenarios for an expected case, best case, and a worse case. However, the more scenarios

---

[1] P. Schwartz. 1996. *The Art of the Long View: Planning for the Future in an Uncertain World* (New York, NY: Currency Doubleday).

that can be developed, the better. Using the correlations and regression models, combined with the standard deviations of the underlying economic variables, one can use a technique called Monte Carlo Simulation to develop thousands of potential outcomes. To develop a Monte Carlo Simulation, a company will build a model for the major outcomes of the firm—for instance, the income statement. For each line of the income statement, it will build in an equation of how that variable is correlated to underlying economic variables. For instance, sales might be correlated to interest rates and GDP growth, while expenses might be correlated to the cost of an input commodity. A computer model can then calculate the sales and costs, and the resulting net income by selecting thousands of possible values for the underlying economic variables using the historical frequency curves for those underlying variables. Thus, instead of creating one or two possible future scenarios, the computer generates thousands of different scenarios or simulations that are consistent with the observed distributions of the underlying variables. The output from a Monte Carlo Simulation is a frequency curve (or table) for the underlying sales, expenses, and net income. Although it sounds very complicated, in reality it is very easy to do and several user-friendly computer packages exist to make the process relatively quick and easy to do.

Monte Carlo Simulation is a very powerful technique for analyzing risk. It shows the distribution of possible outcomes going forward, based on how the underlying variables have performed in the past. Once a Monte Carlo Simulation is set up, it is relatively easy to run different simulations and examine outcomes from utilizing different risk management strategies. This provides a powerful picture of how the future will look, given different risk management strategies.

The fact that the output from a Monte Carlo Simulation is a distribution of possible values is a distinct advantage for the technique. While some managers may prefer to receive a single number for forecasting the future, the reality is that we cannot forecast an uncertain future in such a precise manner. A Monte Carlo Simulation explicitly recognizes this and thus forecasts a distribution of potential outcomes, which is closer to the reality of what we can at best predict. While Monte Carlo does not give a unique answer, it does give a realistic range of answers—that is, a realistic range or distribution of outcomes. It forces managers to think in terms of distributions instead of single numbers, which in our belief is a better way to do the analysis.

There is one main drawback to using a Monte Carlo Simulation. A Monte Carlo Simulation is only as good as the model used to build it, and the distributions used for the underlying economic variables. If a company does not have a good understanding of how its variables of importance such as sales or costs are related to economic variables, then the results of the Monte Carlo Simulation will not be accurate. Likewise, if the relationships change, or if the distribution of the underlying variables change, then the results may be misleading. However, it is also true that if a company cannot model how their operational results are related to economic variables, then any risk management calculation, and any risk management strategy will likely be suboptimal at best. Understanding how the operations of the firm are affected by external factors is an issue of understanding the business, not necessarily a risk issue.

Value at Risk (VAR)

Value at Risk, commonly known as VAR, has become a popular technique that combines many of the principles of Monte Carlo Simulation but distills the results into a single number. VAR was originally developed for financial institutions as a method to give them an estimate of their potential daily losses. Variations of VAR for nonfinancial corporations include Cash Flow at Risk and Earnings at Risk.

With a typical VAR calculation, a Monte Carlo is performed on the forecasted value of the firm (or the forecasted value of the cash flows, or the forecasted value of the expected earnings) and the graph for the distribution of the value if presented. The next step of a VAR calculation is to determine a confidence interval. For financial institutions, this is generally one percent or sometimes a tenth of a percent. For a nonfinancial corporation, a five-percent or a ten-percent confidence level would also be appropriate. For this given confidence level, the value at which there is the probability that the same percentage of forecasted results can then be read off of the distribution graph. This value becomes the VAR. Figure 4.3 illustrates a sample where the confidence level has been chosen to be one percent. In other words, the vertical line is drawn so that one percent of

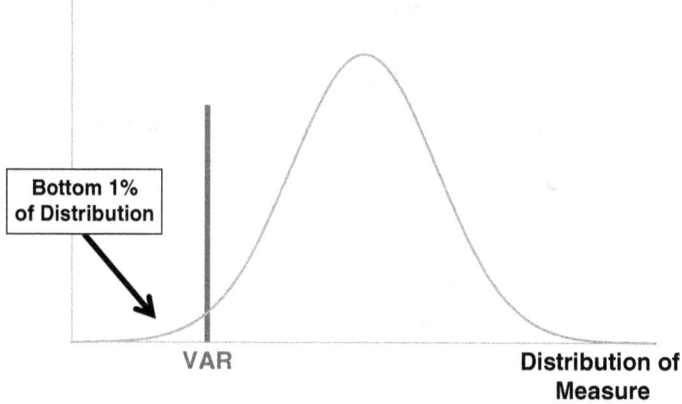

Figure 4.3 Value at risk chart

all simulated values of the variable being measured lie to the left of the line. That value is the VAR.

The VAR calculation is generally done for a given period of time. In other words, the simulation can be done for a day, a quarter, or a year looking forward. Financial institutions usually calculate the VAR for a 10-day period, in part for regulatory reasons. For a nonfinancial corporation, it probably makes more sense to calculate the VAR on a quarterly or yearly basis. Thus, the VAR number is a value of expected downside loss for a given period of time with a given confidence level.

Value at Risk and likewise, Cash Flow at Risk and Earnings at Risk have become popular methods to characterize the riskiness of the firm into a single number. It is a very practical way to examine the usefulness of a proposed risk management strategy as well. The VAR can be calculated assuming no risk management, and again with a variety of different risk management strategies in place. It is one method for calculating the value of risk management by looking at the change in VAR when a risk management strategy is factored into the analysis.

There are a couple of caveats to remember though when using VAR. Firstly, and as with Monte Carlo Simulation, it is a black-box technique in that it is not always possible to back out what the key risk variables are. Secondly, and again in common with the more general Monte Carlo Simulation, it is only as good as the model used to build it. If the managers who build the VAR model do not fully understand and correctly incorporate the economic variables affecting the value of the firm, then the model will give misleading results.

There is also a unique downside to having a single number to characterize the losses that may occur. The VAR measure tells you how much you can expect to lose with a given confidence interval. It is important to understand that it does not tell you how much the loss could be, or what the maximum loss is. Examining Figure 4.2, one needs to realize that there are negative numbers far to the left of the VAR number which represent larger possible loss levels for the firm.

Another unique issue with VAR is that it focuses solely on risk on the downside. Recalling that risk is both the potential for upside gains as well as downside losses, it becomes apparent that VAR is a single-focused measure. For this reason, we prefer to look at the entire results of the Monte Carlo Simulation analysis which shows the entire distribution of upside and downside possibilities. True, the Monte Carlo Simulation does not give you a neat answer as a single number. However, the effort required to examine the entire distribution of results we believe is well worth it.

Dangers of Risk Metrics

Risk metrics are very useful, necessary, and helpful tools for financial risk management. However, financial risk metrics need to be handled with caution as there are some subtle but important inaccuracies and false conclusions that one can make.

To begin this section on the dangers of risk management, consider the reality of what is known as leptokurtosis. There is often an important difference between the theoretical values calculated by the risk quantitative analysts and the realized values that occur in real life. Much of the mathematics used by risk quants is based on the normal distribution. The normal distribution is the bell-shaped distribution that you likely remember from grade school. The normal distribution describes the frequency of various events happening. For many things in real life, it does an excellent job of doing so. Events as diverse as the distribution of heights of a group of people, the distribution of test scores, the distribution of household incomes for a given district, and so on. Given the parameters of the normal distribution, mathematicians can calculate with a high degree of accuracy the number of expected outcomes within a given range.

The normal distribution is also used to calculate the distribution of financial variables and for the most part it works very well. However, it is not perfect. Financial variables are not exactly distributed according to the normal distribution. Most financial variables exhibit what is known as a leptokurtic distribution. In essence, it means that extreme events are more likely to happen in reality than they are as calculated from the normal distribution. Leptokurtosis is also known as "fat-tails," because the extreme tails of the distribution are fatter than theory says they should be. Table 4.1 illustrates using stock returns from the exchange traded fund SPY (also known as Spyders) which tracks the level of the S&P500 Stock Index.

The daily returns for the 20-year period extending from January 2, 1998 to December 29, 2017 were calculated. The first column of Table 4.1 shows the range of "buckets" for returns, while the second column shows the number of days that the actual return did fall into that bucket. The third column shows the theoretical number of returns one should expect given the assumption that stock returns are normally distributed.[2] For the lowest bucket of returns, which represents daily returns below a negative 0.104, we see that there was one day where that occurred in reality, while the theoretical expected number of days that it should have occurred was zero. Likewise, for the largest bucket of returns, those days with a return between 0.124 and 0.136, we see that there was one actual day with a return this large, while the expected number of days from the theoretical calculation is again zero. In fact, the actual number of days with a return below a negative 0.044 is 26 days, while the theoretical number of expected days with a return that negative is only one. Likewise, the number of days with a daily return above 0.052 is 29, while the theoretically expected number of days is only three.

Leptokurtosis is the reason why it seems we have a once-in-a-hundred-year move in the market every few years. It is reasonable to ask why risk quants do not use the leptokurtosis distribution in their analysis. The

---

[2]Technically the calculations were done using the assumption of log-normal distributions. The difference between the log-normal distribution and the normal distribution need not bother us here, and the conclusion is the same regardless of which of the two distributional assumptions are made.

Table 4.1 Daily returns and actual and theoretical frequencies for the exchange traded fund SPY

Return bucket	Actual frequency	Theoretical frequency
−0.104	1	0
−0.092	1	0
−0.080	1	0
−0.068	3	0
−0.056	5	0
−0.044	15	1
−0.032	34	21
−0.020	175	228
−0.008	682	1,013
0.004	2,461	1,855
0.016	1,328	1,409
0.028	234	443
0.040	62	57
0.052	17	3
0.064	8	0
0.076	2	0
0.088	0	0
0.100	0	0
0.112	1	0
0.124	0	0
0.136	1	0

Data for the 20-year period of January 2, 1998–December 29, 2017.

short answer is that there does not exist a mathematical equation to accurately describe leptokurtosis, although it is not from a lack of trying to develop one. For the vast majority of time, the normal distribution works quite well. Additionally, the normal distribution is well known and relatively easy to do calculations with. In fact, the calculations for the above table using the normal distribution were automatically compiled in Excel. The problem is, when you most need an accurate calculation, that is when extreme events are occurring in the financial markets, then that is when the theoretical calculations will be the most inaccurate and misleading. This was the case for the hedge fund Long Term Capital Management (see the case study at the end of the chapter), and this was the case during the lead up to the 2008 financial crisis.

Related to, but not quite equivalent, is the case of Black Swans. A Black Swan is a highly unlikely, but a highly significant event with far-reaching implications. Winning a lottery would be a Black Swan. The events of September 11, 2001 were a rather unfortunate Black Swan. Black Swans are often associated with "fat-tails," but they should be considered to be different in nature. Whether it is Black Swans, or fat-tails, the implication is the same. One needs to be aware of the assumptions underlying the theoretical calculations of risk events.

Before concluding this chapter, there is one more aspect of risk metrics that is not usually considered, but which is critical for proper risk management. Virtually all of the measures mentioned depend on concepts derived from the mathematics of statistics and probability. These mathematical laws depend on having a large number of observations. This leads to what is called the frequency bias, which has subtle but profound implications for risk management.

To understand the frequency bias, consider the flipping of a coin. Assuming it is a fair coin, you know that it will land heads up fifty percent of the time and heads down fifty percent of the time. Thus, if you were to flip the coin one thousand times, you could be relatively confident that it will land heads up approximately five hundred times. If someone was to make a bet with you, whereby they pay you $1,050 every time the coin landed heads and you had to pay them $1,000 every time it landed up heads, you would quickly calculate that your expected value from each flip was $25. If the net payout was to be made after 1,000 flips of the coin, then you would gladly take this bet as your expected value would be $25,000. However, what if we were lazy and only wanted to flip the coin once. If it came up heads, then you would win $1,050,000. However, if the coin flip produced a tail, then you would lose $1,000,000. Now you would likely think very different about how attractive the bet is, even though statistically they are the same. This example illustrates the frequency bias. We calculate outcomes as if we have an opportunity to do them over and over again many times. However, in real life, we generally only have one or two flips of the coin when it comes to a given business decision. Risk managers ignore this fact at their peril.

Case Study
Long Term Capital Management

Long Term Capital Management (LTCM) was a hedge fund that was begun by a group of very seasoned investment professionals and two Nobel Prize winning financial specialists. The Nobel Prize winners were Myron Scholes and Robert Merton. Drs. Scholes and Merton, along with their colleague Fischer Black (who had previously passed away) created the famous Black-Scholes-Merton model for pricing financial options and which underlies many of the principles of financial risk management calculations.

The objective of LTCM was to use financial risk management principles for taking investment risk. The partners of the fund assumed that they would be able to take huge levels of risk, and employ very high levels of leverage to earn outsized returns. They would be able to take huge risks because they would hedge those risks with their Nobel Prize winning risk management models.

For the first couple of years of the fund, the strategy worked perfectly. The fund achieved very high level of returns and it seemed as if risk management was a license to print money. However, things started to unravel just a few years into the life of the firm and ultimately the firm went bankrupt and needed to be bailed out in a rescue operation that was coordinated by the U.S. Federal Reserve.

The example of LTCM shows that model risk and the assumptions of risk management will not always hold; regardless of how sophisticated the analysis. LTCM had a small army of highly trained quants. They had the best of analytical equipment. Ultimately it all failed for LTCM.

There are many lessons to be learned from LTCM. The main one is that models are never equivalent to real-world outcomes, and an undue reliance on models has a high probability of leading to ruin.[3]

---

[3]For those interested in learning more about Long Term Capital Management, an excellent rendering and analysis of the situation are given in the book by R. Lowenstein. 2000. *When Genius Failed: The Rise and Fall of Long Term Capital Management* (New York, NY: Random House).

Concluding Thoughts

Understanding risk metrics is a key skill for everyone involved with risk management. It is not necessarily the calculations that matter—most risk metrics are now done automatically by the data management system in any case. What matters is understanding what the numbers are saying and ensuring that a proper interpretation is being made.

Risk metrics are a powerful and necessary tool for effective financial risk management. However, risk metrics have to be treated with caution. Risk metrics are only as good as the models are to develop them, and only if the mathematical assumptions such as normally distributed variables hold.

Intuition should always be used in conjunction with risk metrics. Remember, financial risk management is as much of an art as it is a science.

CHAPTER 5

Interest Rate Risk Management

Effects of Interest Rate Risk

Variability of interest rates affects a firm in a wide variety of ways. The most obvious one is on the firm's cost of debt. However, there are many other secondary effects in which interest rate affects the financial results of a firm.

As interest rates rise, the cost of equity financing also rises. Additionally, the availability of equity financing diminishes as debt becomes a more attractive investment asset for investors. As debt and equity costs rise, the weighted average cost of capital for the firm will also rise. An increased weighted average cost of capital can significantly alter the strategic plans of the firm by leading to fewer growth projects being accepted and a level of underinvestment overall in the firm.

Relative to the direct costs of debt and equity, interest rates may also affect the availability of financing and the flexibility that firms have in setting the terms and conditions of the financing. This was seen as a prime example during the 2008 financial crisis when even highly rated firms had difficulty securing financing as investors retreated to holding cash.

Many companies also find that interest rates significantly affect demand for the goods and services of their firm. Each firm should have an understanding of its interest rate sensitivity of its sales. Particularly for consumer goods that are typically bought on credit—automobiles as one example—interest costs may play a significant role in affecting sales volatility.

Another direct effect of interest rate changes is the change in credit risk and the potential for bankruptcy; not only bankruptcy of the firm, but also the credit risk or bankruptcy of its customers and suppliers. As interest rates rise, highly leveraged firms come under more scrutiny. The rising potential for bankruptcy has implications for the firm's ability to attract top-level talent, the firm's ability to maintain the faith of its customers, as well as implications for its relationships with its suppliers. This is to say nothing of the direct costs of bankruptcy and the reputational damage incurred.

Management of interest rate risks is thus one of the most common concerns of financial managers and by extension the various stakeholders in the firm. Successful interest rate management helps a firm maintain its good financial health as well as its reputation, which in turn improves its focus on the main strategic objectives of the firm rather than worrying about changing rates which ultimately are out of its control.

Capital Structure Management

The most straightforward mechanism to manage interest rate risk is with thoughtful management of the capital structure of the firm. Maintaining an appropriate capital structure in light of interest rate risk should be a central concern of the financial management—and of the Board. Too often, however, the focus of capital structure is on the current costs of capital or on the accessibility of capital. Although cost and availability are important considerations when developing the capital structure of the firm, they are just two of many concerns that should be taken into consideration. Risk management and flexibility should be given equal weighting when deciding what the next form of capital raising will take. Frequently going for the most expedient lowest cost form of financing can turn out to be very expensive and costly in the long run when risk considerations are taken into account.

The most basic risk concern is debt versus equity as the form of financing. While debt is obviously the less expensive form of financing, the risks of too much leverage and bankruptcy can become all too real, and all too quickly. Higher levels of leverage diminish the financing flexibility of the firm, and particularly so when interest rates rise.

Related to the level of debt financing is the type of debt financing; fixed versus floating rate debt, and short-term versus long-term debt. The cost structures of these two debt financing decisions have a direct relation to the amount of interest rate risk they carry for the firm. Fixed rate debt is obviously less sensitive to interest rates, but because of this lower volatility it also carries a higher average interest cost than floating rate debt. Likewise, long-term debt is also generally more expensive than short-term debt.

Short-term debt has two major components of interest rate risk. The first is the simple fact that short-term debt has to be sourced more frequently. This means that there is a higher likelihood that it may be unavailable when needed. This was certainly the experience of many companies during the 2008 financial crisis when sources of both short-term and long-term debt financing dried up and firms that were financing themselves with short-term debt found it nearly impossible to roll over their debt or refinance with other sources. The second risk is that although short-term debt is generally lower in cost than long-term debt, the variability of short-term debt is much greater than long-term debt. If one examines the historical yield curve, one finds that long-term yields are relatively stable, while short-term yields tend to fluctuate much more significantly. Thus, while short-term debt is less expensive, it adds to the interest rate sensitivity significantly. With long-term debt, the firm will have locked-in its financing. Financing with short-term debt implies that the firm is going back to the market more frequently, and thus will be more exposed to interest rate volatility.

Case Study

Asset Backed Commercial Paper and the 2008 Crisis

The financial crisis of 2007 to 2008 which led to the great recession highlighted many previously unknown or at least underappreciated risks. One such risk arose in the asset backed commercial paper (ABCP) market in Canada, although similar situations were faced in commercial paper markets around the world. ABCP is a short-term debt instrument issued by financial institutions with short maturities up to 1 year, but often for only 30 to 60 days. The issuing entity bundles together, in a special purpose vehicle, an assortment of income generating assets such as credit card loans, mortgages, or auto loans. These assets act as collateral which generally makes these loans very low risk, receiving high credit ratings from ratings agencies, and keeping interest rates low. As the loans mature they are usually rolled over very easily, but unlike traditional bond issues which may have maturities of 5, 10, or even 30 years, ABCP must be rolled much more frequently. Investors buy these securities in part because they are only tying their money up for a month or two. Maintaining investor confidence is critical for issuers of ABCP. In 2007, as the subprime crisis in the United States began to take hold, investors began to avoid mortgage-backed securities (MBS) and soon were shunning anything that may be remotely related to the subprime market. It became difficult at best and at times impossible to value many mortgage- and housing-related securities. As the visibility into the assets within these securitizations is limited, investors were unsure what exposure they may have to subprime mortgages and what this could mean for the value of the securities. Investors at first reacted by demanding higher interest rates on these securities to compensate them for this perceived higher risk, but soon the market for ABCP in Canada froze up almost entirely and it became impossible for issuers to roll over their paper. Without new buyers for ABCP, issuers had very little time to find alternative funding and default appeared likely and would have triggered a disorderly liquidation of the underlying assets, at significantly depressed prices. To avoid this, a plan was created to exchange the short-term ABCP for new securities with much longer maturities of up to 9 years.[1]

In the end, it turned out that Canadian ABCP had a relatively small exposure to U.S. subprime mortgages, but the fear and uncertainty that gripped the market at the time cast a broad shadow over the entire ABCP market. The entire commercial paper market, including securities issued by creditworthy utilities and other firms well outside U.S. subprime saw buyers for their paper disappear, cutting off a crucial source of short-term financing. In Canada, the story had a relatively happy ending; in early 2017, the last of the investors in the restructured notes receiving their

---

[1] T. Perkins. March, 2017. "The ABCs of Asset-Backed Commercial Paper." https://www.theglobeandmail.com/report-on-business/the-abcs-of-asset-backed-commercial-paper/article1053871/

money back.[2] This isn't to say that nobody lost money—after the initial crisis when a market developed for the restructured notes, many original investors sold their holdings at a discount of up to 60 percent from face value, often to hedge funds looking for a bargain.[3]

What lessons can we take from this experience? Firstly, ABCP and other similar products are complicated and often opaque investments. Spending time and effort on appropriate due diligence to fully understand the details of the product and the risks involved can be well worth it. In addition to the individual investment, understanding the market dynamics surrounding the product is important as well. What factors in the market and the broader economy can impact the investment's value or its liquidity, in other words could something happen that would prevent the investor from being able to exit its position quickly without being forced to take a big haircut from fair value. Lastly, issuers of these securities need to be cognizant of market dynamics as well. A firm may be completely confident in the value of the assets underlying ABCP, but when panic hits the market, their securities may be painted with the same brush as paper stuffed with the worst subprime mortgages around. Ensuring that other sources of funding are available should short-term credit markets seize up may prove to be a very worthwhile activity in times of panic.

Know what you are investing in.

Understand the market dynamics and how you can be impacted—even indirectly.

Ultimately, the question of interest rate sensitivity and financial leverage in the capital structure comes down to the business risk of the firm. In this context, business risk is the volatility of the firm's revenues and expenses to overall economic trends. Some firms and some industries are relatively immune from economic cycles—the pharmaceutical industry as one example. Other industries which deal in discretionary goods—such

---

[2]J. Paterson. January, 2017. "What Are the Lessons Learned as Big Investors Finally Get ABCP Money Back?" http://www.benefitscanada.com/investments/asset-classes/what-are-the-lessons-learned-as-big-investors-finally-get-abcp-money-back-92622
[3]Bloomberg News. March, 2015. "How Some Investors Raked in Huge Returns on the ABCP Collapse Wreckage." http://business.financialpost.com/news/fp-street/how-some-investors-raked-in-huge-returns-on-the-abcp-collapse-wreckage

as fashion—are much more sensitive to the economic cycle and thus carry more inherent business risk. As a general heuristic, the greater the business risk of the firm, the less financial risk and interest rate risk the firm should carry through leverage.

Managing Interest Rate Risk

As with most other types of financial risk, there are two main types of instruments for dealing with interest rate risk (beyond the capital structure decisions discussed in the previous section). Firms can use forward type products called swaps, or they can use option type products such as caps and floors. In addition, forward rate agreements (FRAs) and futures contracts that can be used to hedge a one-time interest rate exposure such as an anticipated future debt financing.

Interest rate swaps are a staple of the financial risk manager's tool box. An interest rate swap effectively changes a floating rate liability, such as floating rate debt, into a fixed rate liability. Figure 5.1 illustrates the basic workings of an interest rate swap.

For purposes of illustration, assume that a company has floating rate debt outstanding that is tied to an interest rate index such as LIBOR. Assume that the interest payments on the loan are semi-annual and that the loan has a fixed term of 5 years. Also assume that the firm is paying a floating interest rate of LIBOR plus a credit spread of X basis points. To hedge against the risk of interest rates rising, the bank could enter into

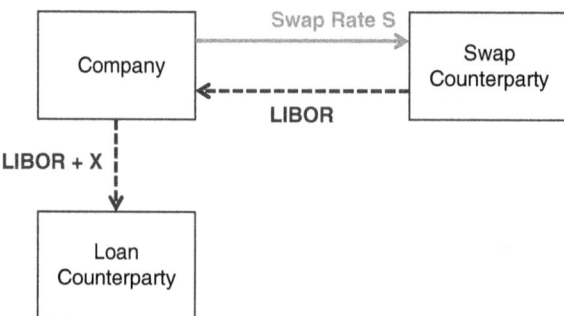

Figure 5.1 Illustration of an interest rate swap

Dashed lines show floating rate payments, while solid line illustrates fixed rate payments.

a 5-year swap with a financial counterparty, and agree to pay a fixed rate S (multiplied by the notional of the swap) and receive a payment based on the LIBOR rate (multiplied by the notional of the swap). The rate S is called the swap rate. The timing of the semi-annual swap payments, as well as the notional amount of the swap, should be set to coincide with the interest payments on the loan.

The net effect of the swap is that the firm is now paying an all-in interest cost of S plus whatever the credit spread X on the loan is. In effect, the company has transformed their floating rate debt into a fixed rate exposure; they have eliminated interest rate risk due to the floating LIBOR rate. If interest rates increase, the increase in the cost on the loan will be offset by the increase in the payments by swap counterparty. However, note that if interest rates decrease, then the company will be making payments to the swap counterparty. As with all forward type products, a swap fixes the exposure so the amount paid is constant. Thus, a swap is a positive when rates go higher, but it is a negative and involves higher net interest costs if rates fall than would occur without the swap.

An alternative to a swap is an interest rate cap. An interest rate cap is effectively like a series of call options on the interest rate. If interest rates rise above a preset level, then the firm will receive a payment from the counterparty. However, unlike with the swap, if interest rates fall, the firm will not have to make payments to the cap counterparty but instead will be able to take full advantage of the fall in interest rates. Figure 5.2 illustrates this.

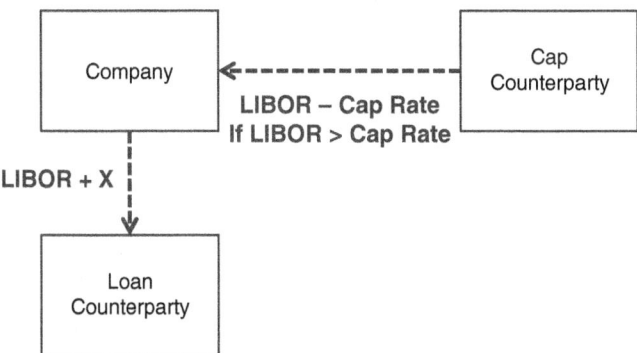

Figure 5.2 Illustration of an interest rate cap

Interest rate cap counterparty makes payment if LIBOR greater than cap rate.

The cap level and the notional amount would be determined upfront. As with the swap, the notional amount would be set equal to the size of the loan. The cap periods, or reset dates, should also be set to coincide with the payments on the loan. For each of the reset dates that the index interest rate is above the cap rate, the counterparty would make a payment to the firm equal to the difference in rates multiplied by the notional amount. This payment could then be applied to the loan payment, thus effectively "capping" the all-in interest cost on the loan at the cap rate plus the credit spread. Note, that if at the reset date the prevailing interest rate is below the cap rate on the reset date, then no payment on the cap occurs. However, in this situation, the firm would be benefiting from lower rates (the rates are below the cap rate), and thus making a smaller interest payment than the cap rate on their loan.

One disadvantage of an interest rate cap is that it involves an upfront cost as it is essentially a series of call options on the interest rate. Generally, an interest rate swap does not involve an upfront cost. To help offset, or potentially totally offset the cost of the cap, a company may choose to enter into an interest rate floor at the same time that they enter into an interest rate cap.

An interest rate floor is like a series of put options on the interest rate. If the interest rate at the reset date is below a specified level, called the floor level, then the company will make a payment to the counterparty equal to the amount that the rate is below the floor level, multiplied by the notional amount of the floor. A company that wishes to buy a cap, can in part, or sometimes in whole, offset the cost of the cap by selling an interest rate floor. This is generally done with the same counterparty that the company has entered into the swap with. The combination of an interest rate cap and an interest rate floor is called an interest rate collar.

For purposes of illustrating an interest rate collar, consider the situation shown in Figure 5.3. For purposes of illustration, assume that the firm has a loan that has an interest rate of LIBOR plus 2 percent. To hedge against interest rates rising, the company decides to enter into an interest rate cap that has a cap rate based on the LIBOR index of 8 percent. To at least partially offset the cost of the cap, the company decides to sell an interest rate floor with a floor rate of 3 percent. The notional

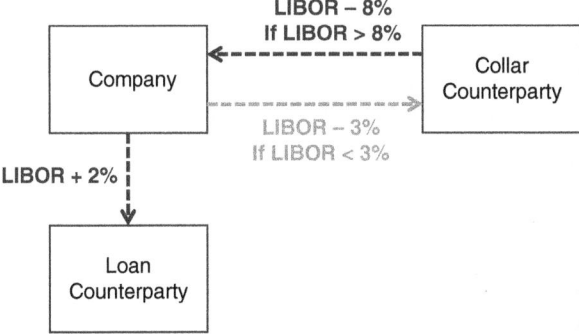

Figure 5.3 Interest rate collar

amount of the cap and the floor is the same as the size of the loan, and the reset dates of the cap and of the floor also match the reset dates of the loan. Whenever LIBOR is above the cap rate of 8 percent, the collar counterparty will make a payment to the company. Likewise, if the LIBOR rate is below the floor rate of 3 percent, then the company will make a payment to the collar counterparty. If the LIBOR rate is between the floor rate and the cap rate, then no payments will be made.

When the collar payments are considered along with the loan payments, then it should be easy to see that the maximum all-in effective interest rate the firm will pay will be the cap rate of 8 percent plus the 2 percent credit spread for a maximum all-in cost of 10 percent. Likewise, the minimum all-in cost that the company will pay will be the floor rate of 3 percent plus the credit spread of 2 percent, for a total all-in minimum rate of 5 percent. Thus, the company has "collared" its all-in effective interest cost between 5 and 10 percent.

After swaps, the next most important interest rate risk management tool is a forward rate agreement. Forward rate agreements, commonly called FRAs, are a forward contract for a specific date. FRAs, like other forward agreements, allow the company to lock in an interest rate over a specific period of time. It is important to note that an FRA is not an agreement to lend (or accept a deposit) at a given rate. Instead, it is a contract that makes a payment between the realized interest rate and the rate that was agreed upon at the inception of the contract. However, this payment, when combined with an actual borrowing will create a locked-in

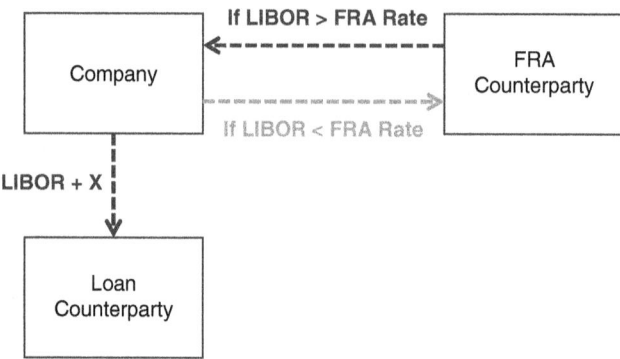

Figure 5.4 Forward rate agreement

rate just as a swap does. Perhaps, the easiest way to think of an FRA is that it is essentially just like a single resetting of a swap. If at the time of the maturity of the FRA, the index rate is above the FRA rate, then the counterparty will make a payment to the company. Conversely, if the index rate is below the FRA rate, then the company will make a payment to the counterparty. The situation is illustrated in Figure 5.4.

Note that the payments of an FRA are a one-time payment. Thus, FRAs are generally used for short-term loans such as loans to cover a seasonal working capital shortfall.

Futures on forward borrowings are also available on the exchanges. The most popular is the eurodollar futures which is a contract based on the 3-month LIBOR interest rate. When buying a eurodollar futures contract, one is conceptually (not actually) agreeing to enter into a lending agreement for a 3-month period. The notional amount is US$1MM. The price of the eurodollar future is equal to 100 minus the yield. Thus as yields go up, the price of the eurodollar futures contract falls. A one basis point change in the 3-month yield implies a change in value of each futures contract of $25 which would be the change for a $1MM borrowing for 3 months if there was a 0.01 percent change in the interest rate; ($1,000,000 × 0.01% × 3/12).

Although eurodollar futures contracts are some of the most frequently traded exchange traded products, they generally are not used by corporations in their hedging activities due to the standardization of the exchange traded product. However, eurodollar futures contracts are heavily used by the financial intermediaries who do offer forward contracts to corporations. These intermediaries use these contracts to essentially engineer the forward contracts they offer to corporations.

The exchanges also offer longer-term futures contracts and option contracts for managing longer-dated interest rate risk. Treasury Bond futures and options are contracts that are based on the theoretical price of long-dated Treasury Bonds, with the most popular being the 5-year and the 10-year Treasury Bonds. Conceptually, when buying Treasury Bond futures or options, one is entering into an agreement to buy the underlying Treasury Bond. Since the value of Treasury Bonds changes with interest rates, the value of the futures contract will also change with interest rates.

Treasury Bond futures and options are generally used to hedge against rising interest rates when the company is considering issuing long-term debt or undertaking a long-term loan. If interest rates rise before the company sources its debt financing, then the value of the Treasury Bond will have fallen in value. In turn, this implies that the value of the Treasury Bond futures contract will have also fallen. The company can thus hedge by selling Treasury Bond futures contracts providing an offset to the increased cost of the debt financing. There are a few caveats when using exchange traded Treasury Bond products. To facilitate trading, there are a few operational details that complicate calculating the appropriate size of the hedge required. Specifically, there are a large number of Treasury Bonds that could be used to satisfy the physical delivery of the futures contracts and this leads to what is known as the "Wild Card Option." The exchange has in place rules, and an adjustment formula, to ensure that all contract holders are treated fairly. The details are beyond the scope of this book, but the reader is advised to check on the details before using exchange traded Treasury Bond contracts.

Exchange traded contracts, both eurodollar contracts as well as Treasury Bond contracts, are useful indicators of expected interest rate volatility. Although they are not perfect indicators of future interest rates (changes in the current interest rate is perhaps a better indicator), the exchange traded contracts do offer an indication of the market's view of expected changes. Knowledgeable risk managers closely follow the futures markets to develop their own sense of interest rate risk.

Concluding Thoughts

Interest rate risk is central to almost any corporation. Interest rates affect an organization's funding costs, and also for many companies affect the level of their sales and their profit margins. Successful management of interest rate risk can provide a significant competitive advantage. There are a variety of ways an organization can manage its interest rate risk. It can do so through the way that the organization chooses to fund itself, or it can do so through the use of derivatives.

CHAPTER 6

Currency Risk Management

Introduction

Currency risk arises from the fluctuations in exchange rates between currencies. Currency trading is the largest trading market with an estimated $3 to $5 trillion being exchanged on a daily basis. Although exchange rate fluctuations are somewhat controlled by central banks, the control has at best a dampening effect and is a secondary factor. Thus, we see wild variations in exchange rates and exchange rate crises such as the Thai Baht crisis in the late 1990s.

Currency risk arises in many different forms. It can be transactional—such as repatriating sales achieved in a foreign currency or paying expenses in a foreign currency, or it can be translational—adjustments to the financial statements based on accounting for foreign currency transactions, or it can be strategic—such as changes in relative price competitiveness to a competitor whose cost structure is based in a different currency.

Relatively few companies will hedge translational exposure. Although it affects the earnings of a company for a cycle, it is not related to cash flows. Most analysts understand the effects of translational exposure and thus are not concerned by the effects on earnings. Most analysts consider that attempting to hedge translational exposure is actually just introducing costs and economic exposure to deal with the cosmetic effects on earnings.

Currency risk affects virtually all companies of a certain size. This is irrespective if a company even has foreign operations or sales. The world operates on a global scale and the relative competitiveness of a company is based in large part on their cost base, which in turn is directly affected by exchange rates. Entire countries, and by extension, entire industries can see their relative competitiveness change quickly as exchange rates tend to be one of the more volatile financial variables. With a robust currency risk management plan, companies can find their competiveness being severely compromised in a hurry.

The markets and techniques for currency risk management are highly developed and liquid. The range of products available for managing currency risk is probably the broadest of any of the financial markets. Due to the high liquidity, currency risk management is also one of the most cost-effective markets to trade in. However, with the breadth of products comes a cost; which is, the extensive range of products implies a bigger learning curve for those companies that want to go beyond the basic forward, swap, and option type products.

Currency Fundamentals

Conceptually, exchange rates are driven by supply and demand just like any other financial product. In large part, this is true in reality, but there are other important forces at work as well. As with interest rates, exchange rates are an important part of a country's domestic economic management policy. Exchange rates affect inflation rates, and also significantly affect employment as a strong currency will make a country's goods less competitive in the global marketplace. If a country's currency becomes too strong, their products become less competitive, which means decreased sales and thus decreased GDP and decreased employment. For these key reasons, central banks keep a keen eye on exchange rate moves and are not shy about using a variety of means to support their currency within a desired trading level relative to other currencies.

For most of the major developed countries, the currency is allowed to "float" or trade freely. Other countries however keep their currency "fixed" within a tight band that is generally pegged to the U.S. dollar. However, even for countries that technically have a free-floating currency, government actions will play a major role in determining the exchange rate or the rate of change of the currency.

Trading levels between countries obviously affect the supply and demand for currencies. Also for those countries that derive significant income from a commodity, the currency can become dependent on that commodity and thus we get the label of a Petro-currency.

Countries through their central banks can, and do, impose a variety of techniques in an attempt to maintain their currency within a desired trading band. The most straightforward is having the Central Bank of the country trade significant amounts of their currency in the open trading markets. Another indirect method that affects the currency is by having the Central Bank adjust interest rates. There is a direct link between interest rates and exchange rates. In extreme cases, countries can affect their exchange rates through currency controls such as limiting foreign currency transactions or even regulating the exchange rate. Both currency controls and regulated exchange rates generally cause extremely distorted markets where official exchange rates bear little to no relationship to actual relative value. When this occurs, black markets for the currency generally arise. In such cases, there will be a demand for "hard currency" from a major developed country that does not have such currency controls.

An example of the demand for "hard currency" was the situation in Russia in the early 1990s as liberalization just started and Western countries were just starting to set up operations there. The Russian Ruble was severely mispriced in the official Russian exchange markets, and thus a black-market exchange market opened up. Many businesses, such as Pizza Hut, would run dual operations; one operation for locals who had Rubles to spend, and a second, and separate set of operations for those who had "hard currency" such as U.S. dollars. While illegal black markets are an option for some risk-loving tourists, they are not a viable alternative for corporations.

There are two central economic relationships that determine exchange rates. The first is Purchasing Power Parity, while the second is Interest Rate Parity. Over the long term, both principles hold quite strongly although there can be short-term deviations for a variety of reasons, most generally trade imbalances, or perhaps even the actions of currency speculators acting on forecasts for relative economic performance of a given country.

Purchasing Power Parity simply says that equivalent goods should cost the same in different countries and in different currencies after accounting for the exchange rate. For instance, if something cost 3 units of currency A, and the exchange rate is 2 units of currency B per unit of currency A, then the cost of the item should be 6 units denominated in currency B.

Case Study

The Big Mac Index

Perhaps the most well-known expression of Purchasing Power Parity is the Big Mac Index that was created by the Economist weekly newspaper. The Big Mac Index tracks the cost of a McDonald's Big Mac burger in a variety of different currencies around the world. If Purchasing Power Parity holds, then the Big Mac hamburger, which is as close as one can get to a completely fungible global consumer good, should have the same cost after accounting for the exchange rate. Of course, the conversion is not perfect, in part because McDonald's does not change the prices of its hamburgers on a daily basis to track currency moves. However, the Big Mac Index does give a relatively accurate, yet quirky, analysis of which currencies are over- or under-valued. It needs to be noted that Purchasing Power Parity is not perfect as taxes, transaction costs, and a variety of other factors will affect the exchange rate.

The second key currency relationship is Interest Rate Parity. Interest Rate Parity states that investing for a set period of time in one period at a fixed interest rate in one currency should provide the same investment outcome as investing in a different currency, and at that second currency's associated fixed interest rate, for the same period of time. In other words, forward exchange rates can be completely explained by interest rate differentials.

Consider the following two-currency example:
  1-year interest rate in currency A is 5 percent
  1-year interest rate in currency B is 8 percent
  Spot exchange rate is 1 unit of currency A = 2 units of currency B

If one has 100 units of currency A to invest, then at the end of 1 year they will have:

$$100A \times (1 + \text{interest rate}) = 100 \times (1 + 0.05) = 105 \text{ units of A}$$

Alternatively, the investor could exchange their 100 units of currency A at the spot exchange rate and receive 200 units of currency B to invest.

Investing the 200 units of currency B for 1 year will provide investment proceeds at the end of the year of:

$$200B \times (1 + 0.08) = 216 \text{ units of B}$$

Thus, the forward exchange rate must be by Interest Rate Parity:

$$105 \text{ A} = 216 \text{ B} \rightarrow 1A = 2.0571 \text{ B}$$

In this case, currency B has depreciated (it now takes more units of currency B to buy 1 unit of currency A). Note that if the 1-year forward exchange rate quoted in the market is anything other than 1A equals 2.0571B, then there will be an arbitrage opportunity and speculators will trade in the currency markets (and the associated money markets) until the Interest Rate Parity relationship holds.[1]

Interest Rate Parity provides a direct connection between interest rates in two countries and the respective forward exchange rates in the two countries. Spot rates, forward rates, and even the respective interest rates will adjust to ensure that Interest Rate Parity holds within a tight band. Therefore, while Purchasing Power Parity holds approximately, Interest Rate Parity is a rule that is forced to hold true due to the actions of arbitrage traders.

Currency Hedging with Operational Strategies

The currency markets for trading and hedging are very active and the number of ways to hedge currency risk with derivatives are many. However, before examining some of the specific currency hedging tools, it is useful to discuss some operational style hedges.

The most basic operational style hedge is to build facilities in the foreign country in which one has operations. Thus a U.S. company that has sales in continental Europe and is concerned about the exchange rate

---

[1] In reality, the relationship for arbitrage is not perfect as we have ignored bid-ask spreads in trading the currency as well as bid-ask spreads in the borrowing/investing rates. Also, currency and investment or borrowing controls may affect the arbitrage relationship.

risk between the euro and the U.S. dollar can build a plant in Europe to mitigate the exchange rate risk. Obviously, there are a host of operational and marketing advantages and disadvantages apart from the currency risk management aspects of taking such an action. There will be a variety of expenses, as well as savings associated with such a tactic, and operational advantages and disadvantages as well.

Hedging currency exposure through developing foreign operations such as building foreign manufacturing facilities is obviously a very blunt way of hedging currency risk. One advantage is that by building foreign facilities, companies will increase their exposure in that country and likely decrease their political exposure. Generally, countries do not want to put local jobs at risk by threatening sanctions, tariffs, or ruinous taxes on a foreign company operating domestically. Countering that point is the risk of expropriation. These concerns are not currency risk per se, but are illustrative of how currency risk management can involve so much more than managing the risk of specific transactions.

From a currency risk management viewpoint, having facilities in a foreign country significantly reduces currency risk as expenses will now also be in the foreign currency. Thus if the foreign currency depreciates, then that implies that the manufacturing expenses will also depreciate on a relative basis. To the extent that expenses and sales are related, there will be a natural hedge.

A second operational hedge is to set up the financing in the foreign currency. By taking on debt in a foreign currency, one now has obligations in a foreign currency that help to offset the cash inflows in that currency, thus reducing the currency risk. A related benefit of financing in a foreign currency is that one may also be reducing the sovereign risk of an expropriation or of currency controls. If the cash outflows are restricted, then the company may be able to justify not making payments on debt denominated in the currency of that country and debt that is held by investors in that country.

A third operational hedge that is used in business-to-business transactions is simply to sell globally in your own domestic currency. This essentially puts the currency risk on the foreign buyer. Obviously this has disadvantages as it may negatively affect sales, but in countries without a convertible currency, or one that cannot be easily hedged, it may be the only method to reduce or eliminate currency risk.

Several companies have taken currency risk and turned it into a marketing advantage by giving business-to-business clients the choice of currency in which they may pay. If a company has strong currency risk management capabilities, this is one method that they can use it for competitive advantage. By giving the customer the choice of currency in which to pay, an organization is essentially taking on the currency risk management for their customer. In many cases, this may be a service that the customer would be happy to pay for, or at least give preferential sales considerations to.

Operational strategies such as building a manufacturing capability in a foreign country tend to be very blunt long-term tactics for currency risk management. The use of traded derivatives is better suited for specific situations and is of course easier and more flexible in nature.

Currency Risk Management with Derivatives

As with all other types of financial risk, there are two main types of instruments for managing currency risk: forward type strategies and option type strategies. Again, as previously discussed, forward type strategies lock in the price at which the transaction will occur, while option type strategies allow one to asymmetrically manage good risk versus bad risk.

There are a couple of unique challenges when developing hedging strategies for currency risk. The first challenge is that currency risks are arising on a daily basis as the company may have an uneven and random stream of both cash inflows as well as cash outflows in a variety of different currencies. The fact that currency transactions occur on a more frequent basis than, for example, interest rate risks tied to a financing which tend to occur less frequently, implies that it is more complicated to calculate the exact amount of exposure at any given point in time. Additionally, there is the aspect of cash inflows, as well as outflows which adds to this challenge. The exact outstanding net balance of exposures to a given currency can be a constantly changing dynamic. At any point in time, a company could have either a net long exposure to a foreign currency or a net short exposure to a given currency.

The second difficulty of currency hedging is that there are likely to be several currencies that the organization is exposed to. These currencies will have varying correlations. At any given point in time, the domestic currency could be strengthening against one foreign currency and depreciating against a second currency. The currency exposures to the two foreign currencies could be offsetting at any given point in time. Hedging both of them simultaneously without taking into account the correlation between the currencies could in fact lead to a case of over-hedging, where the net effect is that the company, based on its hedging activities, has not neutralized its exposure to changes in the exchange rate, but actually magnified it. The difficulties of precisely hedging currency risk have given rise to the use of exotic options for managing currency risk. Exotic options will be discussed later in this section.

For specific foreign currency transactions, the most straightforward way to manage is with a forward transaction or an option transaction specifically tied to the size and timing of the transaction. For a company with relatively few foreign exchange transactions, this is probably the simplest and most effective method to manage currency risk. Managing currency risk on a transaction-by-transaction basis, however, does not deal with the issue of the strategic aspect of currency risk, nor is it practical for a company that has a large number of ongoing foreign currency transactions.

In such cases, the use of currency swaps or captions is probably more appropriate. To calculate the notional amount of swap needed, it will probably be necessary for the firm to build a model of its expected cash inflows and outflows over the proposed life of the swap. To incorporate the strategic risk of currency changes, it should also try to model the price elasticity of its sales to changes in exchange rates.

Modeling of the notional amount of a currency swap needed is not a trivial task and it is likely that several heroic assumptions and forecasts will be needed. Thus, it is probably best to use the currency swap as a base hedge and frequently monitor its effectiveness. Forwards and options can then be used to make adjustments throughout the life of the swap as model assumptions change and correlations between currencies change.

Like all derivatives, currency derivatives can be cash settled or physically settled. In a cash-settled currency derivative, the exchange rate difference is paid in units of the domestic currency. Conceptually there is not a difference between physically settling a derivative transaction or having it cash settled. However, for currency swaps that have exchange of physical, there is a significant difference in the amount of counterparty risk and thus it is worthwhile to take a look at the mechanics of a currency swap that involves exchange of notional at the beginning and at the termination of the swap.

For a currency swap that has exchange of principal, there is basically a three-step process. Consider the example of a 5-year swap of US$50MM for €41.5MM. Assume that the floating legs of the swap are U.S. dollar LIBOR and Euribor, respectively, on a semi-annual basis. The U.S. counterparty will receive Euribor and there will be an initial exchange between the two counterparties of US$50MM for €41.5MM as shown in Figure 6.1.

For the 5-year life of the swap, the swap payments based on the two floating interest rates will be made as shown in Figure 6.2. The U.S. counterparty will make payments based on a notional of €41.5MM and the Euribor rate, while the euro counterparty will make payments on a notional of US$5MM and based on the U.S. dollar LIBOR rate.

In the final step, the principal amounts will again be exchanged, only this time, with the currency flows going the other way as shown in Figure 6.3.

Figure 6.1 First step of a currency swap with physical exchange of notionals

Figure 6.2 Interim swap payments

Figure 6.3 Final exchange of notionals

An issue is that over the 5-year life of the swap, the U.S. dollar and euro exchange rate could have changed quite significantly. This potentially leaves quite a large counterparty exposure for each of the counterparties. In an interest rate swap, or a commodity swap, the counterparty exposure actually decreases as the swap nears maturity. For a currency swap with exchange of principals, the counterparty exposure actually increases. For this reason, currency swaps can also be completed, but without the exchange of principals at inception and at maturity of the swap.

Case Study

Caterpillar

From mines in Australia to construction sites in Alabama, few sights are more ubiquitous than the heavy machinery of Caterpillar, painted yellow with the contrasting black "CAT" lettered prominently. The world's leading manufacturer of construction and mining equipment, in 2016 Caterpillar generated total revenue of $38.5 billion primarily from three segments: construction industries, resource industries, and energy & transportation.[2] Approximately three-fifths of its revenue comes from countries other than the United States, with Caterpillar dealers serving 190 countries.[3] Operating a global corporation provides many benefits in terms of diversification of revenue, but also presents challenges in managing exposure to fluctuations in foreign exchange. When operating outside of the United States, much of Caterpillar's revenue will be denominated in the local currency—pesos in Mexico, euros in Spain, or dong in Vietnam—but Caterpillar's earnings are reported, dividends are paid, and interest on much of its debt is paid, in U.S. dollars. In addition, its operating expenses will be in a wide array of currencies. As global exchange rates fluctuate, Caterpillar's earnings, in U.S. dollars, will fluctuate as well.

How does Caterpillar manage its foreign exchange risk? In its 10-K filing, Caterpillar states

---

[2]https://www.caterpillar.com/en/company.html
[3]Caterpillar. "Caterpillar Inc.: Overview." http://s7d2.scene7.com/is/content/Caterpillar/CM20171201-48288-53810

Machinery, Energy & Transportation operations use foreign currency forward and option contracts to manage unmatched foreign currency cash inflow and outflow. Our objective is to minimize the risk of exchange rate movements that would reduce the U.S. dollar value of our foreign currency cash flow. Our policy allows for managing anticipated foreign currency cash flow for up to five years.

This short statement contains a great deal of information about its foreign exchange hedging including what is being hedged, the objective of its hedging program, what financial products are used, and the time frame over which the risk is managed. By managing its currency risk in this manner, Caterpillar is sending a message that when an investor purchases shares in the company, they are investing in the operational core competencies of the company—e.g., manufacturing and selling heavy machinery—without being completely exposed to fluctuating foreign exchange rates. Another dimension of foreign exchange risk that Caterpillar must be mindful of is that as an exporter, a strengthening U.S. dollar makes its products more expensive to foreign buyers (in their local currency).

Although Caterpillar is an extreme example operating in 190 countries, in today's increasingly global marketplace, almost all medium and large enterprises (and even many smaller ones) will have some exposure to exchange rate variability. After identifying its currency exposures, a firm must decide whether or not to hedge this risk, and what tools to use if it does choose to hedge. Caterpillar provides an excellent example of a large company with significant foreign exchange exposures that has implemented a broad hedging strategy.

Currency swaps are also frequently used for financing purposes. A company may have a funding need for one currency, but have a funding need in a second currency. Assume that our U.S. counterparty in the previous example had a need for €41.5MM, but was having difficulty securing euro financing at attractive rates. Also assume that the company was able to secure financing in U.S. dollar easily and at a U.S. LIBOR rate that was acceptable. The U.S. counterparty could thus secure financing in U.S. dollars, and enter into a physically settled currency swap. The three steps of the currency swap would then be as follows.

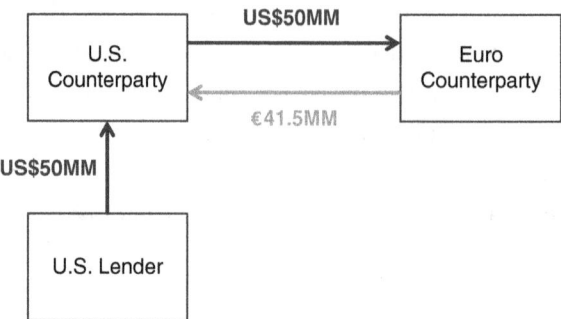

Figure 6.4 Currency swap combined with domestic borrowing

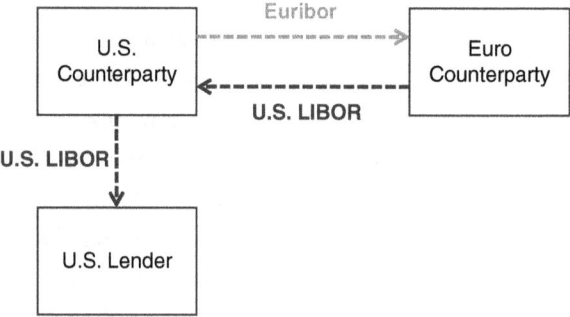

Figure 6.5 Interim swap payments

Figure 6.4 shows that the U.S. counterparty is borrowing US$50MM and immediately swapping it for €41.5MM. The net cash flow for the U.S. counterparty is a cash inflow of €41.5MM.

Figure 6.5 shows the interim cash flows over the 5-year life of the swap. It is also assumed that the terms of the loan are also 5 years on a semiannual basis and that the swap dates are set to be equivalent to the interest payment dates on the loan. At each loan interest payment, the amount of the U.S. dollar payment is offset by the cash inflow of the U.S. dollar payment from the swap. In turn, the net payment by the U.S. counterparty at each payment date is simply the euro payment on the swap.

Figure 6.6 shows the maturity payments. The maturity payment of US$50MM on the loan is offset by the US$50MM received from the swap payment. The net payment by the U.S. counterparty will be the €41.5MM payment on the swap.

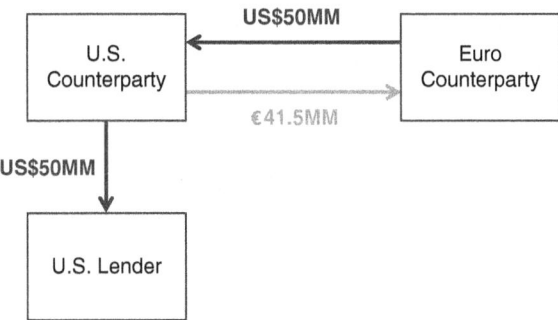

Figure 6.6 Currency swap maturity payments

Thus at inception, the U.S. counterparty receives a net payment of €41.5MM. Interim payments over the 5-year life of the transactions are that the U.S. counterparty makes a semi-annual payment of Euribor on €41.5MM. At maturity, the U.S. counterparty makes a net payment of €41.5MM on the swap. Notice that the net payments are exactly as if the U.S. counterparty had executed a €41.5MM loan. In essence, the U.S. counterparty has synthetically created a euro-based loan through funding at advantageous rates (and presumably with more ease) in the U.S. loan market and entering into a currency swap. If the U.S. counterparty has euro-based sales receipts, they have effectively hedged these receipts through the use of the synthetic euro loan. If the euro depreciates, then so will the net payments that the U.S. counterparty needs to make on the swap. Note, however, that this analysis does not account for any sales elasticity due to exchange rate fluctuations. If the euro depreciates, it will make the U.S. company's products more expensive in euros, which in turn may negatively affect sales.

Before leaving the subject of currency swaps, it is important to note that the previous example in which a U.S. company borrows in U.S. dollars and then swaps for euros can also be used to gain a funding advantage. Large multinational companies will canvas global markets to find the currencies in which they can most attractively get funding. They then use the above strategy of currency swaps to swap into the currency in which they actually want to use the currency. In doing so, they get attractive funding, and they get currency risk management. This is a very popular tactic for companies that are comfortable with using and executing currency swaps.

Earlier in this section, some of the specific difficulties of managing currency risk were mentioned; namely that a typical company will have a large number of foreign currency transactions, and additionally that it is likely to have exposure to several different currencies with differing correlations. Both issues make the calculation of the exposure and of the amount of foreign exposure to hedge quite challenging. To overcome these difficulties, there are a couple of exotic derivatives that are frequently employed in hedging currency risk.

Average Rate Options, also called Asian Options, calculate the payment based on an average of the rate over a period, rather than the exchange rate on a given date. Average Rate Options have several advantages. Firstly, they are not tied to a specific date and thus the concern about having a mismatch between the date in which a foreign currency transaction is done and the date on which the hedge is calculated is reduced. If a company has a series of cash transactions occurring over the month, it can enter into an Average Rate Option and achieve a hedge payout based on the average exchange rate over the month. While this is not a perfect hedge, it closely approximates the average rate at which the company will be transacting in the foreign currency. A second advantage of Average Rate Options is that they are generally much less expensive due to the calculus of pricing these options.

A second type of exotic option that is useful for hedging currency risk is a Basket Option. In a Basket Option, the payout is based on how the currency performs against a basket of foreign currencies. For instance, you could buy a hedge on the U.S. dollar versus a basket consisting of the euro, the British pound, and the Canadian dollar. In essence, the payout of the Basket Option is based on the average performance of the U.S. dollar versus these three currencies. Over the life of the option, it is likely that some of these currencies would have appreciated against the U.S. dollar and some would have depreciated. Thus, the payout of the Basket Option will be muted based on the offsetting effects of the appreciation of some and depreciation of the other currencies, but this muted payout will match the exposure of the company doing the hedging. Like with the Average Rate Option, the pricing of the Basket Option will be less expensive than entering into a series of equivalent conventional options on the three currencies. The averaging effect again reduces the implied volatility, and also reduces the expected total payout, but also matches more closely the actual exposure that the company is facing.

As with all exotic options, the pricing is nonstandard, more difficult, and involves more assumptions. This means that different dealers are more likely to have different prices and thus it pays to do some due diligence and ensure that one entering into these more advanced transactions is getting a fair transaction price.

Concluding Thoughts

While all financial risks can affect a company both in terms of their transactions, as well as in terms of their strategic competitiveness, currency risk has the greatest potential to affect the competitive position of a company relative to its foreign-based peers. Fortunately, the currency market is very large and very liquid. Thus, there are a plethora of financial tools and strategies that firms can use to not only manage this risk, but also use it to gain a competitive advantage.

Exchanges rates, and more accurately, changes in exchange rates are directly tied to changes in the relative interest rates between two countries. This effect, known as Interest Rate Parity, gives rise to unique financing opportunities, whereby a firm can use currency derivatives to not only manage currency risk, but also potentially gain a funding cost advantage.

CHAPTER 7

Energy Risk Management

Introduction

As with all other aspects of financial risk management, managing risk associated with energy markets is both an art and a science. Standard quantitative techniques and risk management practices are certainly applied, but the finer nuances of energy markets—from spikes in real-time electricity markets to price spreads between various grades of heavy fuel oil—make energy risk management a particularly interesting and at times challenging endeavor.

Energy use has been closely tied to economic growth since the industrial revolution when burning coal as a fuel to produce steam became common in England, eventually spreading across the globe. Although coal is still widely used in electricity production and steelmaking, other fossil fuels such as natural gas and oil, nuclear power, and renewables are now all important sources of energy. Each of these energy sources has unique characteristics that contribute to the particularly challenging nature of energy risk management.

Although no single precise measurement of total energy expenditures exists, estimates for the earlier part of this decade range from US$5 to US$6 trillion or close to 10 percent of global GDP.[1] This is an astounding amount of money, and managing risks in these markets is critical to the success of individual companies and the economy as a whole.

Not all companies are equally exposed to energy markets, and varying degrees of sophistication within an energy risk management program is expected and appropriate. The degree of exposure can be classified into three broad categories:

---

[1]Leonardo Energy. November, 2016. "World Energy Expenditures." http://www
.leonardo-energy.org/resources/798

- *Primary*: companies whose primary line of business is in the energy industry—oil and gas exploration companies, oil refiners, and energy marketers. The financial success of these companies is highly dependent on energy prices, and therefore they are likely to have robust and sophisticated risk management programs to specifically identify and manage exposure to energy risks.
- *Secondary*: companies that are not directly in the energy industry, but that have significant exposures to energy markets. Examples include energy-intensive manufacturing companies, mining companies, and airlines. These companies tend to also have robust risk management programs to manage energy risk, but often as a component of their broader financial risk management systems and practices, as opposed to a standalone risk management program.
- *Tertiary*: companies with minimal direct exposure to energy markets. Technology, retail, and restaurants are examples of businesses in this category. These companies often do not put much thought into directly managing their energy risks. While other risk factors tend to have a larger impact on their financial success, energy costs can still be a meaningful input cost and should not be ignored.

Energy Price Risk

The most direct exposure to energy markets faced by many firms is to the level of energy commodities: for example, oil, gas, and electricity. Energy markets tend to be volatile and in certain circumstances can exhibit extreme volatility. The primary reasons for this volatility are the physical nature of energy commodities, limited transportation capacity to deliver energy from its source of production to point of consumptions, and the limited ability to store energy in many forms, which result in supply/demand imbalances. One of the most extreme examples of volatility in energy markets occurs in real-time electricity markets. In deregulated electricity markets such as New York, a System Operator receives offers from power generators to sell electricity and will dispatch power plants, and imports from neighboring markets, in an attempt to match supply to demand in a reliable and low-cost manner. When the system is nearing its maximum capacity, typically on hot summer days when air conditioning load is high, the unexpected loss of a power plant due to operational issues can result in a shortage of supply causing massive price spikes in the market price of electricity which updates every 5 minutes. Generally these price spikes are very short-lived as new supply will come online and price-sensitive demand will reduce their usage helping to quickly bring the market back into equilibrium (Figure 7.1).

On July 20th, 2017, prices for the New York City zone printed 5-minute intervals as low as $24.29 and as high as 1,438.41/MWh; a range that would be unthinkable in most markets. Granted, this is an extreme example and very few companies are directly exposed to this particular risk, but it does serve to demonstrate key risks which are paralleled to lesser degrees in natural gas, oil, and other energy markets.

Over longer periods of time, energy markets can be subject to boom-and-bust cycles, often in line with broader economic cycles. As economic activity picks up, demand for energy often increases more quickly than supply can be added, leading to increasing prices. The higher energy prices lead to greater investment in exploration and resource development, but the time it takes to bring incremental supply to market means that often this supply hits the market as the economy is losing steam and even entering a recession. The combination of decreased demand and increased

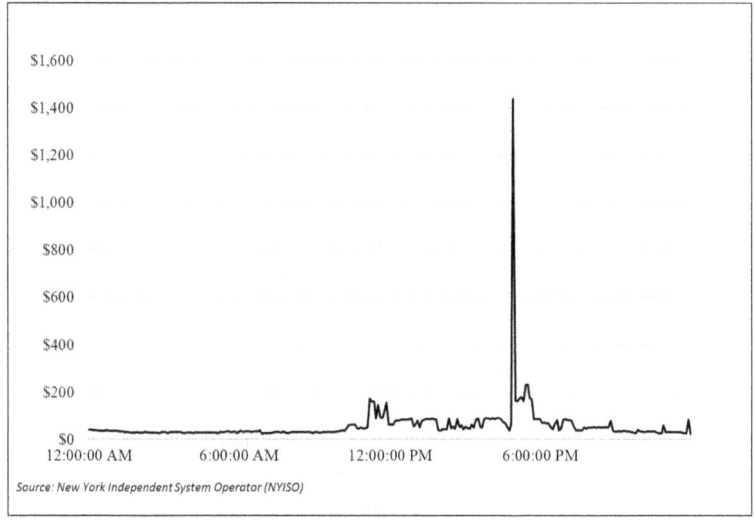

Source: New York Independent System Operator (NYISO)

Figure 7.1 NYC real-time power prices, July 20, 2017

supply can lead to drastic decreases in energy prices. It is important for a risk manager to understand the connection between economic cycles and energy prices, and of course how the financial performance of their firm is connected to both energy prices and economic cycles.

In addition to understanding the factors that influence prices of each energy source, there are some particular nuances of energy markets that can create significant differences within fuel types, which we explore in the following sections.

Basis Risk

Basis risk is a familiar concept in many financial markets and can refer to the deviations between a spot price and a futures contract price, or more generically between a financial hedge and the underlying exposure. In energy markets, there are additional dimensions that must be monitored: locational basis and quality basis.

Locational basis refers to differences in the price of the same commodity in different places. For example, natural gas in Boston is (almost) chemically identical to natural gas in Louisiana or Korea, but the price of this gas may be very different at the same time. This arises from the fact that natural gas cannot be transported freely and instantaneously around the world like a currency transfer or an interest rate can be in digital form. This same feature of energy markets arises in varying degrees in all physical commodities, particularly in those which are difficult and costly to transport, or where sufficient infrastructure does not exist to bring production from its source to where it is consumed. Oil production in the western Canadian oil sands has increased significantly over the last decade; however, pipeline capacity to bring this production to refineries or export terminals has not kept pace. At times, this leads to a significant discount for oil sands production. This is very different from financial commodities such as currencies: US$1 may cost €1.1 in New York and at the same time will trade at practically the same level in Tokyo, London, and Singapore. Many deregulated electricity markets have locational marginal pricing where hundreds or thousands of locations within a single state or multi-state market will have different prices. These prices are comprised of three components: an energy component that is uniform across the entire market, a loss component to reflect the energy physically lost through the transmission of electricity, and a congestion component that reflects the fact that limited transmission capacity will mean the next available lowest cost source of supply cannot always be used to meet demand at all locations and a more expensive source of supply may need to be used. At times of peak demand when many transmission lines are nearing the maximum capabilities, significant congestion can occur causing major differences in prices at locations that may be very close together geographically but on opposite sides of the transmission constraint.

Quality or product basis refers to different quality characteristics within an energy type that can lead to pricing differences. Coal is a prime example, as depending on where it is mined, it can vary across a number of quality characteristics: heat content, sulfur content, mercury levels, and even its hardness to name just a few. Depending on how these characteristics vary, the price of two otherwise indistinguishable coals may be very different. Higher heat content means a lower volume of coal must be consumed to produce the same amount of electricity and is therefore likely to trade at a higher price. Sulfur content in coal when burned is released as an air pollutant, which makes it an undesirable characteristic. Coals with lower levels of sulfur will tend to trade at a premium to higher-sulfur coals. Metallurgical coal, or "met coal" is used in steelmaking, whereas thermal coal is used for electricity production. The unique characteristics required for steelmaking, such as high heat content and low levels of impurities, means that at times met coal can be much more expensive than thermal coal.

Oil can also exhibit similar product quality dynamics: heavy, sour crudes tend to trade at a discount to light, sweet crude; however, this depends significantly on the relative supply of each type and the availability of refining capacity capable of handling each type. Once oil has been refined, quality differences can still result in price differentials: heavy fuel oil for sale in New York Harbor that contains 1 percent sulfur typically trades at a premium to 2.2 percent, which in turn trades at a premium to 3 percent. As financial hedges are not liquid for every product type and quality, it is important for the risk manager to understand how these basis differentials can change over time, what factors influence these differentials, and how to most effectively use available financial hedges to mitigate exposure to related but not perfectly correlated products.

Case Study
American natural gas markets

For a deeper dive into locational basis risk, we can explore American natural gas markets, where in certain regions during periods of high demand the pipeline infrastructure is insufficient to meet the needs of consumers. This can result in price spike in the daily gas markets, and significant price separation between production areas and key market areas. For example, the U.S. Northeast region consumes a large quantity of natural gas on cold winter days for power generation, industrial uses, as well as significant volumes for residential and commercial heating needs. Prices in the Northeast can decouple from those in the rest of the continent, spiking higher in constrained areas where pipeline infrastructure cannot deliver enough natural gas to meet demand. The higher prices incent price-sensitive consumers to reduce their demand: natural gas fired power plants will be replaced by generators that use other fuels, or plants capable of burning oil will switch to this alternative fuel, and some industrial consumers will temporarily halt some optional processes. The ability for consumers to reduce consumption or switch to alternative fuels is in itself a very valuable form of operational risk management that can replicate some of the effects of buying financial hedging products. North American natural gas futures contracts that trade on exchanges such as the Intercontinental Exchange (ICE) or the New York Mercantile Exchange (NYMEX) are settled at Henry Hub, a pricing hub in Louisiana located near the major production basin in the Gulf of Mexico. If natural gas transportation infrastructure was sized such that production could always reach every consumption area, prices would be much more uniform across the continent, and natural gas could be hedged simply with Henry Hub futures. Unfortunately, pipeline capacity is limited and the resulting constraints cause price separation between Henry Hub and the key demand centers which can make Henry Hub futures ineffective hedges if you are located downstream of the constraints. Luckily there are other products, basis swaps (or futures), that can be used to hedge the locational differential. A purchaser of a natural gas basis swap pays a fixed price and receives a floating price equal to the difference between price at the location referenced in the contract and Henry Hub, as illustrated in

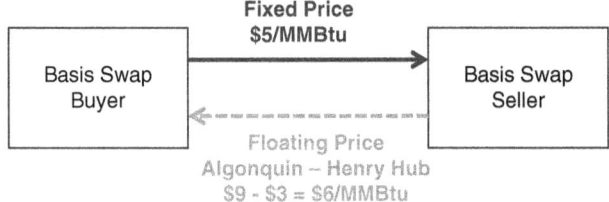

Figure 7.2 Basis swap

Figure 7.2. When prices rise in the market area relative to Henry Hub, the swap purchaser receives the difference which offsets the higher price paid for the physical natural gas they are consuming. A gas consumer in New England may enter a swap for January where they pay a fixed price of $5/MMBtu and in return will receive the difference between the monthly index price for Algonquin Citygates and the price at Henry Hub. If Algonquin settles at $9/MMBtu and Henry Hub at $3/MMBtu, the swap buyer will receive a net payment of $1/MMBtu.

Seasonality

Unlike financial products like stocks and bonds, which effectively trade the same regardless of the weather outside, certain energy commodities can exhibit significant seasonality, with prices and volatility spiking at times of high demand. This is shown in the New York electricity and Northeast natural gas examples cited earlier in this chapter. A key operational risk management tool for some companies is to reduce consumption when prices are higher; however, this real option is not available to all market participants. For example, a natural gas local distribution company (LDC) must supply gas to its customers, generally at a fixed price, regardless of what price they have to pay for the gas. What makes this risk particularly dangerous is that the amount of gas these companies must supply is highly correlated with prices: higher volumes on days when market prices are highest. LDCs, and other companies facing similar risks, use a portfolio approach to mitigate exposure to these risks including physical and financial contracts, as well as investment in infrastructure. LDCs often contract for firm pipeline capacity which allows them to import natural gas from areas of supply where prices tend to be lower, allowing them to avoid paying the higher prices in the market area. They often enter into physical supply agreements with producers or marketing companies at a fixed price, eliminating exposure to volatile market prices. Other physical contracts may be indexed to trading hubs, which leaves exposure to market prices that can be mitigated through the use of financial derivatives. Some physical contracts contain swing options, allowing the purchaser flexibility in the volume purchased for a given day or month, allowing the company to better align its purchased volume to what it must supply to its customers. Physical storage is another very valuable risk management tool, where a company can inject natural gas into a storage facility at times of low pricing and withdraw it when prices are high, helping minimize purchases at times of peak pricing.

Each of these risk management tools has a cost, whether through an option premium paid to a marketer or fixed demand charges paid for pipeline or storage capacity. Many companies have some ability to pass hedging costs through to their customers, but a decision must be made as to how much risk should be mitigated and how much is acceptable for the company or its customers to bear. Managing broad exposure to large market movements may make sense as it can be done using standard products with high liquidity and low costs, but entering into highly customized bespoke contracts with financial institutions to manage risk that may not be material to the overall business may not provide a level of risk reduction commensurate with the costs incurred. This decision is a key part of any company's risk management process and will need to consider all the internal and external objectives and pressures unique to each firm.

Geopolitical Risk

Although we have explored several instances of market dynamics related to localized environments and infrastructure constraints, energy markets are also influenced by global trends and events. Much of global oil production occurs in regions that have been prone to armed conflict or general geopolitical instability including Iran, Iraq, Saudi Arabia, and Libya. Conflict, the threat of war, terrorism, sanctions, or regime change can either directly reduce oil production or raise the possibility of future supply disruptions, leading to increases in prices and volatility. The wars in Iraq, the Arab Spring movement, and sanctions imposed on Iran are all examples of geopolitical risk. The increase in liquefied natural gas (LNG) trade has had the effect of turning natural gas into more of a fungible global commodity; however, not to the extent of oil or coal. The increase in LNG exports from more stable countries such as the United States and Australia also helps dampen geopolitical risk in the natural gas markets.

Legislative and Regulatory Risk

Due to its critical role in the economy, and even national security, the energy industry is often subject to a high degree of regulation and is exposed to regulatory and legislative risk. This may be at a local, state or provincial, national, or even international level. One example is in natural gas pipeline development in the United States, where in a constrained region like New England, the addition of a major interstate pipeline would have a significant impact of pricing. Although the Federal Energy Regulatory Commission (FERC) has overall jurisdiction over approving interstate pipelines, states can block pipeline development by refusing to grant water permits, and local governments can refuse to allow siting of infrastructure such as compressor stations. At the federal level, pipelines may or may not receive approval from FERC, a decision which can drastically impact forward market pricing in these regions.

Environmental legislation can also have a major impact on energy markets, particularly over longer time periods. This may take the form of local air pollution rules which limit the use of certain fuels, or from global agreement like the Paris Agreement which seeks to reduce greenhouse gas emissions globally to limit further global warming. A number of tools can be used to reduce greenhouse gas emissions; for example, jurisdictions may ban through legislation the use of carbon-intensive fuels like coal, they may provide tax credits or other incentives for the production of renewable energy, or they may require electricity providers to source a certain percentage of their supply from renewable sources through the implementation of Renewable Portfolio Standards. Each of these tools will impact energy markets in unique ways, and it is important for the risk manager to monitor enacted and proposed legislation and regulation to understand the potential impact to their business directly or more broadly to energy markets to which they are exposed.

Application of Hedging Tools

Similar to other financial risks, futures, swaps, and options can be used to hedge energy price risk. Futures contracts are available on many energy contracts; however, much of the liquidity is concentrated in only a few key contracts. Although many other contracts exist, the vast majority of financial oil derivatives trade on two contracts: West Texas Intermediate (light, sweet crude delivered to Cushing, Oklahoma) which serves as a benchmark for crude in North America and Brent Crude, a North Sea product which serves as a benchmark for global prices. Many consumers of oil may not be directly exposed to changes in either of these benchmarks, but rather they consume refined products: heavy fuel oil, gasoline, diesel, or heating to name a few. Futures contracts are also available on these refined products; however, the liquidity tends to be limited, especially for longer-dated delivery. Some basic quantitative analysis such as regression analysis can help identify which energy indices are most correlated to a company's earnings or other key financial metrics. It is important to be mindful of the competitive landscape and whether or not energy price changes can be passed on to customers. This type of situation was explored in more detail in Chapter 2 with the Southwest Airlines Case Study.

Returning to our definition of risk, the possibility that good or bad things may happen, will lead us to our next decision: whether to protect against only one direction of price movement while leaving the company exposed to opposite price movements, or to hedge exposure to price movements in both directions. Simply, should we eliminate exposure to "bad things" while allowing the company to benefit from the "good things" or eliminate exposure to both the bad and good things? If minimizing exposure to both upside and downside risk, financial products that lock-in a price, such as swaps, forwards, or futures contracts are a natural choice. For buyers of these contracts, an increase in the market price of the reference asset will result in gains which offset the rising cost of the physical energy commodity, while a decrease in the price of the reference asset will result in losses. Regardless of the direction of market movements, entering these contracts has the result of locking in the price paid. There are relatively liquid financial markets for many energy commodities; however, these contracts tend to reflect only the most common qualities and only for a limited number of delivery locations. These risks were discussed in greater detail earlier in the chapter, and market participants must be mindful of how their energy costs may not be perfectly correlated to the available financial products.

If a decision is made to hedge only one side of the risk, options are a natural choice. For example, an energy consumer who buys a call option will be protected from rising prices by receiving a payoff from the option as prices rise, but as prices fall the option expires with no obligation for either party to make a payment, so the buyer is able to benefit from the lower market prices in the physical market. Options of course require an upfront payment to the seller, namely the option premium. Option prices are higher for more volatile underlying assets, and energy commodities tend to be more volatile than many other financial assets, making using options to hedge a very expensive proposition at times. In addition, options are more complicated, therefore requiring more sophistication in the risk management department, and tend to be much less liquid than futures contracts.

Physical contracts can also be a very effective risk management tool in the energy industry. By entering into an agreement with an energy supplier to purchase electricity, gas, oil, or any other fuel, the buyer is removing much of the basis risk discussed earlier. The exact product is known, the delivery location is known, and depending on the nature of the contract even the price may be known. These contracts can be structured to allow for volume flexibility eliminating some of the volumetric risk faced by energy consumers. For many smaller consumers of energy, these are the only contracts needed. They buy their electricity from the regulated local utility under a set tariff, and their natural gas comes from the LDC, again under a regulated tariff. These tariffs, however, typically only eliminate price risk over short periods of time: the tariffs will be updated on a periodic basis (typically annually, but at times more frequently) as the cost of service incurred by the utility changes. As fuel costs are typically the largest and most volatile single component of this cost, entering into financial hedges to offset changes in these tariffs may be required for companies wishing to manage energy price risk over longer time periods.

Trends

Users of electricity and natural gas need to be mindful of long-term trends that influence broader market price levels. These trends can be driven by many factors such as an increased focus on climate change or technological innovation which makes hydrocarbon reserves economically accessible.

Energy markets are highly dynamic, and it is important for risk managers to be mindful of new and emerging trends, both regional and global, which may have a significant impact on prices and volatility. Energy production is the primary contributor to global greenhouse gas (GHG) emissions, and the increased focus on climate change is causing major changes to the way in which energy is produced and consumed. Renewable energy sources such as wind, solar, and hydro are increasing in importance with production costs for solar photovoltaic electricity in particular experiencing huge decreases in cost. Intermittent sources of generation, which unlike traditional fossil fuel based generation (ignoring maintenance outages) cannot always be counted on when needed and sometimes produce surplus electricity when it cannot all be consumed. One way to solve this issue is through the use of energy storage. Battery technology has been an area of research and development, and a few large grid-scale storage projects have been placed in service recently, but although falling, the costs are still relatively high. As prices continue to fall, more batteries will be deployed which will allow integration of additional intermittent renewable generation.

Another key trend over the last decade has been the use of hydraulic fracturing and horizontal drilling to access previously uneconomic oil and natural gas reserves. These technologies have been widely adopted in the United States, resulting in a reversal in the long-term decline in oil and gas production, and significantly reducing American reliance on imported hydrocarbons. The increased natural gas production has resulted in depressed pricing and a reduction in volatility. This has resulted in somewhat of a renaissance for U.S. manufacturing and petrochemical industries as well helping continue the shift from coal-fired electricity to natural gas. It has also resulted in some consumers of natural gas incurring large losses on their hedging programs leading to a complete re-thinking of their hedging activities as exemplified in the Florida Utilities Case Study in Chapter 10.

Risk Management Process

It is important to develop a solid understanding of how your firm is exposed to energy markets either directly through energy purchases and sales or indirectly through the knock-on impact on production inputs or shipping costs. Once exposures have been identified, a determination must be made as to whether or not these exposures can be hedged: what physical or financial contracts or operational decisions are available that can mitigate these exposures? Next, a decision must be made as to how much, if any, of this exposure should be hedged depending on the particular situation of the firm in the context of its financial profile and competitive position in its industry. Then develop an execution plan and enter the hedges. The final step in ongoing monitoring and reporting of risks and the overall hedging program, a step that is ongoing and will result in an iterative process as new and changing risks are identified, new hedges become available, or the financial profile and objectives of a firm evolve over time.

Concluding Thoughts

From traditional manufacturing firms to technology companies with massive data centers or cryptocurrency miners, energy will continue to be a critical component of the global economy. Each energy type presents unique challenges, from natural gas pipeline constraints causing locational basis risk to political unrest in the Middle East increasing volatility in the oil markets. Many standard financial derivatives are available for use in energy risk management, but physical contracting practices and operational hedges are also invaluable tools for risk managers. Understanding the nuances of highly dynamic energy markets will allow firms to create robust risk management plans and make informed and prudent hedging decisions to support financial objectives.

CHAPTER 8

Credit Risk Management

What Is Credit Risk Management?

Credit risk management is managing the risk that financial obligations are met, or not met as the case may be. There are two aspects of credit risk management. There is the internal aspect of credit risk management, which is insuring that the organization has the financial wherewithal and financial flexibility to meet its outstanding as well as potential outstanding financial obligations. The second aspect is external credit risk or ensuring that the customers of the organization are able to fulfill their financial obligations and debts to the organization.

Internal credit risk management is important as it firstly affects the solvency and long-term viability of the organization. There are very real costs of bankruptcy or distressed financial health that are both explicit as well as implicit. Bankruptcy is expensive legally and financial stress leads to higher financing costs, loss of customer loyalty, difficulty in keeping and attracting good employees, worsening of relationships with suppliers, a loss of financing flexibility, and a resulting level of underinvestment that prevents the company from remaining competitive in its industry.

External credit risk management is a balance between extending credit to customers in order to enhance or maintain sales and a positive relationship and goodwill against the possibility that payment may be delayed or even not forthcoming. Credit policy is frequently a major component of the marketing package. Consider the financing packages used by automobile manufacturers or furniture dealers and how it plays to their marketing strategy to attract new customers and maintain existing customer relations.

Both the internal credit risk as well as the external credit risk need to be managed. However, in this book, we will focus on the external credit risk management and leave the internal credit risk management to the financial management books. However, the metrics used for external credit risk analysis should of course be used to monitor one's own credit risk. Having an understanding of how one might be viewed by others is prudent risk management.

Credit risk management is one of the financial risks that the firm often neglects or pays insufficient attention to until it is too late to develop an effective plan. In part, because of this we often see credit risk arise as a systemic event as it was during the 2008 financial crisis. It takes only a small sector of the economy to start defaulting—or even to have an increasing risk of default—for cascading effects to occur that affect large parts of an industry or even an economy.

Like all financial risks, credit risk tends to be dynamic. It is well known that overall in the economy that companies, and indeed sectors of the economy, tend to get weaker financially than they tend to get stronger. This implies that credit risk needs to be reevaluated on a regular basis. It is most certainly not a one-time event, although due to the nature of how personal credit works—for instance, credit cards—the instinct is to assume that once one is considered to be an acceptable credit risk that one will always remain an acceptable credit risk.

There are a couple of ways though in which the nature of credit risk differs significantly from the other financial risks covered in this book. The first is that credit risk has a definite cut-off—namely that the firm suffers a credit event in which it fails to meet a financial obligation; you are either in default or you are not. For all other financial risks, prices can move more or less to any level up or down. With a definitive credit risk, there is basically a zero—one effect. The firm can be meeting its financial obligations or it is not. This is highlighted when a firm goes bankrupt. While a firm can obviously be in better credit health than its peers or in worse credit health than its peers, the reality is that in the eyes of business law, a firm is either meeting its credit obligations or it is not. There is a close analogy with a biological organism; it is either alive, or it is dead. There is no Schrödinger Cat like phenomenon where an entity can be a certain percentage bankrupt, although admittedly there are different levels of financial distress.

A second difference is that credit risk is frequently considered to be a one-way risk; credit risk is for all intents a bad risk with only very limited upside potential. With all of the other financial risks discussed so far, there is a possibility that the risk could be a good risk (prices move in one's favor), or a bad risk (prices move against one's favor). With a few minor exceptions, credit risk can only be bad. For example, it is rare to find an organization with financial obligations paying back *more* than they are legally obligated to.

This leads to the third difference of credit risk which is in regards to the correlation of credit risks. As has already been discussed, financial risks tend to be correlated. This is true for credit risk as well, but only to a certain point. The correlation of credit risks can have some unusual and counter-intuitive outcomes. The first is the difficulty of uncovering when the credit risk of an organization is an idiosyncratic event or a systemic event. An organization could be in financial distress due to systemic factors or due to totally idiosyncratic factors. However, even if financial distress is a function of systemic factors, the correlation can change suddenly for one or more of the correlated firms. Take for instance the case of GM and Ford during the 2008 crisis. The credit health of both firms deteriorated in a highly correlated fashion as the crisis began to spread and endure. However, when GM filed for bankruptcy, the credit risk of Ford counter-intuitively improved. The cause of this was that as one of the major competitors found itself handcuffed (temporarily) by filing for bankruptcy, that in some sense gave Ford more freedom to exploit whatever market opportunities there were at the time and actually improve its probability of not going bankrupt. Thus, while one of the highly correlated companies filed for bankruptcy, the credit correlation reversed course and the two companies for a while became inversely correlated in their respective credit risks.

There is a final element that distinguishes credit risk. It is a difference that is frequently overlooked, in part due to its subtleness. Credit risk is frequently caused by an unforeseeable event or a series of unforeseeable events. For instance, with the exception of the issuance of credit cards (which are analyzed and assessed in an entirely different manner), financial institutions almost never extend credit to a counterparty that they expect to fail. Financial institutions understand that in the aggregate that they will experience credit losses, but for each individual credit they extend credit to they do so only if they are highly confident that the credit will be repaid. Thus, when a credit event does occur, it is almost always because of an unexpected event or a series of events. We expect financial prices to go up or down; we do not expect creditors to fail, yet of course we know that they do.

This subtle difference has major implications for analyzing credit risk. Since credit events tend to be unique and specific to the context, we have to be very careful in applying traditional probability-based techniques. It is related to the frequency bias that was discussed in Chapter 4. The mathematics of determining who will go bankrupt is different and the mathematical nature of the losses is also different from the other financial risks. The losses from credit risk are sudden and large; they are not a matter of degrees like they are with other financial risks. For instance, a small interest rate move may imply a small change in financial position while a large interest rate move will likely imply a larger change in financial position. With credit risks it is either no loss, or a loss. Furthermore, if it is a loss, then it generally is a significant loss. It is a subtle difference but one that has profound effects for how one measures credit risk effects, and makes the task of pricing credit risk far more difficult.

In terms of financial risks, credit risk may be one of the simplest to comprehend, perhaps because it is the one that almost everyone deals with in their day-to-day personal lives. However, the fact that it is considered simple to understand does not mean that it is easy to master. Credit risk may be one of the subtlest of the financial risks, and this in turn makes it one of the trickiest to manage well.

Credit Derivatives

In the mid-1990s, a new type of derivative called the credit default swap was developed. Credit default swaps dramatically changed the world of credit analysis and gave traders a way to trade, and thus price pure credit risk. When trading a bond, you are in essence trading the underlying interest rate of the bond, plus the associated credit risk, or credit spread on the bond. The reason that bond price changes are thus not always a good way to assess credit risk is that the change in the interest rate component inherent in the price of the bond was generally of much greater magnitude than the change in the level of credit risk. The rise of credit derivatives changed all of that and provided an instrument whose value depends solely on credit risk.

The credit default swap is the basic building block of credit derivatives. In a credit default swap, the credit protection buyer pays a periodic fee, generally semi-annually, to the credit protection seller. The credit protection seller in return makes a payment to the protection buyer if, and only if an underlying reference credit, generally linked to a corporate bond, suffers a credit event such as a default or a bankruptcy. The size of the payment is based on a notional amount multiplied by 1 minus the recovery rate on the reference asset. Figure 8.1 illustrates this.

So for illustration, assume that the credit default swap was based on a notional amount of $10MM. Also assume that 3 years into the 5-year swap that ABC went bankrupt and the resultant price of their bonds that were trading at 37 percent of face value, which would indicate that investors expected to recover $0.37 for every dollar that they were owed. In this case, the protection seller would make a payment to the protection buyer of $6.3MM ($10MM multiplied by 1 minus the recovery rate of 37 percent). In this way, the protection buyer has protected themselves from a default of ABC company.

Credit default swaps provide a very simple and straightforward way to hedge credit risk. A side benefit of this market is that market forces are setting the credit default swap price. As a company's credit health deteriorates, the price for buying protection through a credit default swap will increase. Likewise, as a company's credit health improves, the price of a credit default swap referenced to it will decrease. Thus, the credit default swap price on a company is a very timely and relatively accurate way to assess the credit health of a company.

Figure 8.1 Credit default swap

Credit Risk Metrics

Besides credit default swaps, there are a wide variety of credit risk metrics that can be used to assess the financial health of an organization, or even a person. The first concept to understand about credit risk is the difference between credit exposure and expected loss due to a credit event. Exposure is the size of the outstanding credit. It is the size of the loss one would experience if there was a credit event and nothing was recovered in terms of payment from the counterparty. For credit obligations such as a loan, calculation of the exposure is simply the size of the loan outstanding. However, with other credit-related obligations such as derivative contracts with counterparties, the potential exposure is uncertain, as the size of the future net derivatives payments is generally unknown. In such cases, the exposure is generally taken to be the maximum expected size of the credit obligation.

The expected loss on a loan is the multiple of two components: the expected loss given a credit event and the probability of a credit event occurring. The expected loss given that a credit event has occurred can be a function of many different factors. The primary factor though is the value of the collateral. That is why it is relatively easier to get credit to buy a house. A house acts as very good collateral, so if there is a default, the lender can seize property that will have significant value and thus the expected loss given a default will be low. Conversely, this is also why you generally cannot get consumer credit on perishable goods.

To assess credit, one of the first variables to look at is a company's credit rating, or a person's credit score. The credit rating of a company gives an overall view from an independent source (the credit rating agency) of how likely it is that a creditor will receive full payment on their credit extension. Generally, credit ratings of BBB or better are considered to be "investment grade" or relatively safe, with a BBB-rated company having less than a 0.2 percent probability of defaulting within a year.[1]

There is a major caveat with corporate credit ratings; ratings tend to be relatively sticky. Rating agencies for a variety of reasons tend to be loath to change ratings. To avoid having to change ratings every time

---

[1]S&P Ratings. www.spratings.com

economic conditions change, rating companies examine a company over an assumed business cycle. This evens out possible fluctuations due to changing business conditions, but it also implies that ratings may be misleading if economic conditions are poorer than usual.

One interesting side fact about credit ratings is that the rating agencies take into account the strength of a company's risk management systems as part of their ratings analysis, which gives corporations yet another reason to practice good risk management.

Altman Z-Scores

A second method to assess the credit quality of a company is to examine what is known as their Altman Z-score. The Altman Z-score was developed by the academic Edward Altman. In his analysis, he looked at a variety of factors and developed the following equation and set of factors:

$$Z\text{-score} = 1.2 \times F_1 + 1.4 \times F_2 + 3.3 \times F_3 + 0.6 \times F_4 + 0.999 \times F_5$$

Where:

$$F_1 = \frac{\text{Working Capital}}{\text{Total Assets}}$$

$$F_2 = \frac{\text{Retained Earnings}}{\text{Total Assets}}$$

$$F_3 = \frac{\text{Earnings Before Interest and Taxes}}{\text{Total Assets}}$$

$$F_4 = \frac{\text{Market Value of Equity}}{\text{Book Value of Debt}}$$

$$F_5 = \frac{\text{Sales}}{\text{Total Assets}}$$

If the calculated Z-score is below 1.80, then there is a high probability of the company encountering financial distress. If the Z-score is above 2.99, then the company is considered to be a safe credit risk. Values of the Z-score between 1.80 and 2.99 are considered to be indeterminate in terms of credit quality.[2]

Related to the Altman Z-score which is used for corporate credits are credit scoring techniques for individuals. Like the Altman Z-score, these proprietary credit scores take into account a wide variety of different factors including past payment history, level of education, length of time in a given residence, and a host of other factors. Credit scores are based on statistical techniques and do not necessarily take into account the specific situation of a given individual.

The Five (Six) Cs of Credit Analysis

One credit analysis technique that examines the specifics of a company is what is known as the five Cs of credit analysis, which was heavily used by bankers in the past. To this list, many financial institutions have added a sixth factor. These factors are: (1) Character, (2) Capital, (3) Capacity, (4) Collateral, (5) Conditions, and more recently, (6) Compliance.

Character can simply be stated as the willingness of the counterparty to pay. Certain companies, and indeed certain individuals, develop a reputation for being slow to pay or finding reasons to not pay or dispute the size and terms of the payment. Experienced credit officers will tell you that character is by far the most important of the analysis of credit risk that they perform. Bankers in particular will tell you that they would rather deal with a borrower with good character and poor capacity to pay, than one with a perfect capacity to pay but poor character. When dealing with large organizations, character is often less of a factor unless it is a tightly controlled firm with a dominant personality in control. Character becomes more of an issue with smaller firms, where there is more likely to be such a dominant individual who sets the tone for the firm in dealings with counterparties. Ironically, as credit analysis has come more under the auspices of big data, the role of character has regrettably taken a diminished role. Character is assessed through personal relationships or

---

[2]E. Altman. September, 1968. "Financial Ratios, Discriminant Analysis and the Prediction of Corporate Bankruptcy," *Journal of Finance* 23, no. 4, pp. 189-209.

more likely through the credit and payment history of the organization. The one caveat of relying on history to assess credit character is that true character can only be truly assessed in times of stress. It is generally quite easy to have good credit character if one has never had financial stress.

Capital involves the analysis of the existing financial reserves of an organization. Obviously, the larger the financial reserves, the smaller the credit risk of an organization is likely to be. Capital is related to the old joke of the bank being more than willing to lend you money when you don't need it, but loath to lend when you most need the money.

Capacity is the ability of the firm to pay. Although many financial ratios are used to assess capacity to pay, the most important metric for measuring capacity is perhaps the coverage ratio, or the ratio of cash inflows to the firm divided by the required cash outflows required to keep the organization in good credit standing. The debt-to-equity ratio is also a key component. In particular, the debt-to-equity ratio relative to industry peers. Common wisdom tells us that companies in the same industry should face similar growth opportunities and similar levels of risk and thus should have similar debt-to-equity ratios. It is considered a red flag if a company has a much higher debt-to-equity ratio than its industry peer group.

Collateral is what can be recovered if the counterparty cannot pay. The presence of collateral makes the granting of credit for certain purposes much easier. For instance, household mortgages are quite easy to secure as there is readily available collateral. A liquor store, however, is far less likely to be extended credit as the assets are far less collectible after they have been used.

Conditions are the state of the economy or the industry at the time that the credit question is being posed. As with many financial variables, there are cycles to credit; namely, there are times when the economic conditions are prime for credit and during such times credit is readily available at attractive prices. Conversely, there are periods where the economic conditions in general, or the conditions for a specific industry are far from ideal and during such times credit is much more expensive to obtain, or perhaps unobtainable at any reasonable cost. During the height of the financial crisis this was certainly the case, when even the most financially secure of companies had difficulty obtaining credit financing as investors preferred to hold cash given the level of economic uncertainty.

To these traditional five components of credit analysis, many lenders, and in particular financial institutions, have added the sixth metric of compliance. In large part, this is a reaction to regulatory concerns placed on financial institutions in the wake of the events of 2008. However, it also makes sense as it relates to not only regulatory compliance but also issues such as reputation, cyber security, and even strategic risk. For instance, no one wants to be accused of extending favorable credit terms to a criminal organization or a terrorist organization.

Together, the five/six Cs of credit risk determine to whom one might extend credit and the extent of that credit. Once the decision has been made to extend credit, the next step is to develop a credit policy.

Developing a Credit Policy

The credit policy of a firm is the conditions under which the firm will extend credit to its customers. Components of a credit policy include; (1) whom to extend credit to, (2) how much credit to extend, (3) the terms under which the credit will be extended, (4) how the credit will be monitored, and (5) what will be done if the credit terms are not fulfilled.

The terms of credit are not only a credit risk decision but also a financial cost decision. Extending credit has an explicit cost as the organization that is extending the credit has to; (a) source the financing for the credit, (b) pay for that source of financing, and (c) pay for the additional monitoring costs of monitoring the credit. Obviously, the terms of the credit risk need to take into account the sales effect versus the need to offset the cost of financing the credit extension.

In determining whom to extend credit to, a company will generally establish a minimum level of credit quality. This could be based on credit rating, credit score, maximum credit default swap price, or an internal credit analysis based on the five Cs of credit. It is also likely at this step the company will have tiers of credit quality that they will extend credit to, with better tiers of credit quality being granted larger amounts of credit and at better credit terms.

Once the decision has been made to extend credit, the next step is to determine how much credit to extend. The extension of credit, and the amount of credit extended can have a major impact on sales. Generally, the amount of credit to extend is a function of the credit analysis, the size of the customer and their ability to service the credit, and how much sales activity the customer is likely to have. Generally, the better the credit rating, the greater the extent of credit will be.

The terms of the credit are essentially what implied interest rate on the credit will be. Again, this could be a function of the credit rating of the customer, the extent of credit granted, or a function of both factors. One does not want to act as a major competitor to the bank for the customer, and also one needs to keep in mind the costs of financing the credit. Ultimately, the terms of the credit may come down to a marketing decision, with the implied costs of extending the credit implicitly charged to the cost of sales or embedded in the sales price.

The one key aspect of extending credit to clients is in monitoring the credit. This is generally done by monitoring the days receivable, and acting on any credit payments that are past due.

A final component of the credit policy is what to do when a customer cannot, or will not, make payment. This is an often neglected part of credit policy, but one that it is much better to plan for in advance, rather than when it is necessary to put such plan into action. The usual strategy is to have a series of escalating notices and then warnings. However, when that does not work, other action may be taken including taking legal action or hiring a collection agency. Each of these actions has different ramifications that may reflect badly on the organization that puts them into practice.

In total, credit risk management involves a lot of moving parts, yet is often critical to sales success.

Concluding Thoughts

Credit is one of the most visible financial risks, yet one of the ones that we still have the most trouble accurately assessing and establishing accepted best practices for managing. Credit management, both one's own credit as perceived by the external stakeholders, as well as the credit granted to customers, is a key component of the day-to-day managing of a business.

The development of the credit derivative market has revolutionized the assessment of credit and how credit risk is managed by financial institutions. It is likely that some of these techniques will be filtering to the general-use market in the next few years.

Meanwhile, consumer credit is likely to be affected by big data techniques, in part based on social media activity, so new developments in consumer credit can also be expected in the near future as well. It is an exciting time to be working as a credit risk analyst!

CHAPTER 9

Commodity Risk Management

Introduction to Commodity Risk Management

By this point of the book we have covered many of the factors and the techniques for managing financial risk. The last area we will cover in this brief chapter is commodity risk. Commodity risk is the risk caused by the volatility of commodity prices. Commodities are generally grouped into two categories: agricultural commodities and metals. To this list we will also add weather—yes, it is possible to manage the economic effects of weather.

There are a couple of aspects that make managing the price risk of commodities unique. The first is that a much larger percentage of trading in the commodity markets is being done by market participants who actually want (or need) to use the commodity for some end purpose. In other words, they are trading the product for the use of it, not simply for the direct economic gain from trading activity. For instance, the cereal manufacturer is buying corn, not because they believe the price of corn is going to rise, but because they need the corn to produce the breakfast cereals that they are in business to manufacture and market. The interest rate markets, the currency markets, and the credit markets in particular are markets in which the majority of trading activity is for direct economic gain. Although hedge funds in recent years have begun activity in trading commodities, the number of individual investors or portfolio managers examining their retirement portfolios and thinking about corn or palladium prices is very small. This means that supply and demand are a much more important factor in determining the price volatility of commodities than are the actions and perceptions of speculative traders.

A second unique aspect of commodities is that their price tends to trend, that is, the prices of commodities tend to take long turn swings either up or down, and once commodity prices start to move in a particular direction, then they tend to stay trending in that direction. This implies the use of exotic derivatives to take advantage of this fact. Note, however, that this trending is not always the case, and a change in circumstances can quickly cause a trend in the opposite direction.

A third unique aspect that commodity derivatives share with energy is that they cannot be stored and transferred digitally like interest rates or currencies can be. Thus physical delivery, transportation issues, location issues, and overall basis risk are much more important factors.

A fourth difference that exists with commodity derivatives is that they are highly dependent on the weather. Severe weather changes can drastically alter the price forecasts for certain agricultural products. It is interesting to note that while most traders have a screen in the trading room showing the business news, commodity trading rooms always have the news screens turned to updates on the global weather.

A final difference is that some nonfinancial corporations are actually in business to take on commodity risk. This is particularly true for commodity producers such as farmers or mining companies. The issue of commodity price risk becomes one of whether they should hedge or not hedge. If they are in business to produce the commodity, then it may be the case that investors want them to take the exposure and are expecting them to take the exposure. However, if price level prospects for the commodity are dim, or if the price volatility of the commodity is too great, then not hedging may put the company into financial peril. Managing commodity price risk is thus a strategic decision for these companies. Whatever the decision on risk management is, the issue is to ensure that the decision is clearly communicated to the relevant stakeholders.

Case Study

Barrick Gold

From Egypt to India to Peru, gold has long been valued in many cultures around the world for its beauty, with gold jewelry acting as a key indicator of social status. It has also been used for centuries in coins as a direct measure of wealth, and even with the advent of paper money, for a long time many of these bank notes were convertible into gold by the holder. Gold is also used in industrial applications due to its conductive properties. Despite its central place in cultures past and present, all gold ever mined on Earth would fit into a 23-meter cube![1] In 2016, the world's largest gold producer was Barrick Gold Corporation, with total production of 5.5 million ounces.[2] Barrick is headquartered in Toronto, Canada, and has mining operations around the world, although its core operations are primarily in the Americas.

One of the most basic strategic decisions for any gold producer is whether or not to hedge its output. Selling production forward provides guaranteed revenue, dampening volatility arising from changing market prices. At one extreme, hedging 100 percent of production for the upcoming years by selling futures or forward contracts will eliminate all exposure to gold market prices—they will not benefit from rising prices, but will not be harmed by falling prices. The opposite is true for firms that choose not to hedge any of their production. Many investors purchasing the shares of a gold producer do so because they are looking for exposure to gold prices; therefore choosing to hedge may make a producer much less attractive to a set of investors.

Barrick Gold provides a great example of a firm that has changed its hedging strategy. For years Barrick was firmly in the hedging camp, but in 2009 they shifted their strategy, deciding to limit additional hedges and unwind much of their existing hedge portfolio. As gold prices rose through the 2000s, gaining momentum as the financial crisis took hold in 2007 and 2008, Barrick's hedge portfolio began to show significant liabilities as forward market prices were much higher than the prices at which Barrick had entered their hedges. The company was incurring significant financing charges related to these positions, but more troubling for the company, shareholders were unhappy as Barrick shares underperformed smaller unhedged competitors. Late in 2009, Barrick announced an equity issue of up to CAD$4 billion with the proceeds intended to unwind its

---

[1]World Gold Council. https://www.gold.org/about-gold/facts-about-gold
[2]V. Basov. March, 2017. "World's top 10 Gold Mining Companies—2016." http://www.mining.com/update-worlds-top-10-gold-producers

9.5-million-ounce hedge portfolio. This addressed the concerns of shareholders, but came at a steep cost as the additional equity caused dilution of existing equity holders. The immediate reaction to the announcement was negative with shares falling 6 percent; however, there were positives for Barrick as Charles Oliver, a portfolio manager with Sprott Asset Management stated: "I wanted to own gold companies and not companies involved in the hedging business" and that he "may have to revisit the Barrick story."[3]

Barrick's financial hedges worked as they anticipated, reducing exposure to market prices and guaranteeing the net revenues to be generated from their gold sales. There was no fraud, and no issues of inadequate controls or management oversight. Yet Barrick made the strategic decision to abandon its hedging program and leave its revenues exposed to variable market prices. There is no "right" or "wrong" answer to whether Barrick should have made this change, but for strategic purposes at the time they felt it was the right direction for the company to take. The answer to this strategic question will be different for different firms and even for the same firm at different times. The most important takeaway from this story is the importance of understanding both the internal financial reasons to hedge or not to hedge, and also the external requirements by shareholders, debtholders, analysts, and other stakeholders, and arriving at a decision that considers all of these potentially conflicting requirements.

Basis Risk

Basis risk is the risk that the price changes in what you are hedging, for example jet fuel prices, is not exactly the same as the price changes in the financial contracts or instruments that you are using to managing the risk, for example oil price forward contracts. As an example, see the case study of Southwest Airlines in Chapter 2. Basis risk was also a key element in energy risk management as discussed in Chapter 7. For energy risk, the basis risk was in large part based on location, in that energy prices had different prices in different locations.

---

[3]A. Hoffman. September, 2009. "Why Barrick Reversed Its Gold-Hedging Strategy." https://www.theglobeandmail.com/globe-investor/investment-ideas/why-barrick-reversed-its-gold-hedging-strategy/article4287614

Basis risk is a major issue in commodities as well. To begin, there is the location issue. If one is hedging oranges, one may need the physical oranges. Having the oranges located in a different part of the country is not going to help if one needs to start a production run of orange juice today. Secondly, like most commodities, not all oranges are identical. Again, as in energy where it was discussed that not all oil is equivalent, likewise not all oranges are equivalent. This is quite different from trading interest rates, where the 30-day LIBOR rate for any given day is a fungible rate that is consistently applied on a global basis.

In the presence of basis risk, knowledge of the correlation between price changes in the underlying and prices changes that are referenced in the hedging instrument is key (again, for example, Southwest Airlines using oil price contracts to hedge jet fuel prices). One needs to ensure that the correlation is stable, and that the correlation is high. Any change in the correlation will diminish the effectiveness of the hedge.

One way to manage basis risk is through a basis swap. A basis swap is just like a traditional swap, only the two counterparties will trade the difference, that is, the basis between two reference indices. For instance, it may have been possible for Southwest Airlines to hedge the basis risk between jet fuel prices and oil prices by entering into a basis swap of the market price of jet fuel for the market price of oil as shown in Figure 9.1.

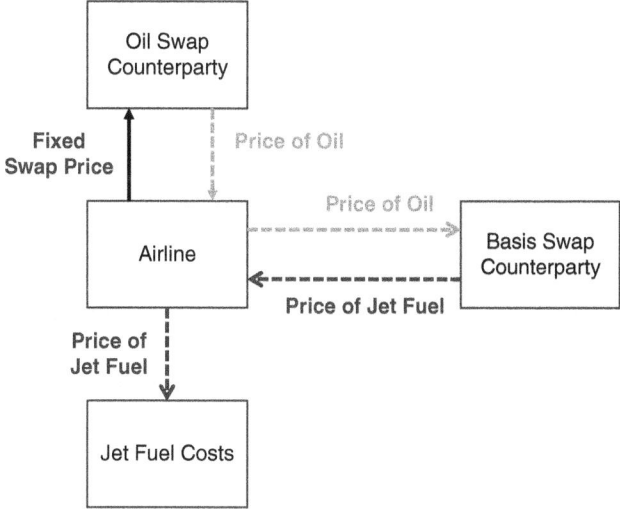

Figure 9.1 Illustration of basis swap

At the reset dates of the swap, the airline will pay the counterparty the market price of oil on the reset date (multiplied by the notional amount), and in return receive the market price of jet fuel (multiplied by the notional amount). By combining a basis swap, with the more readily available oil price swap, Southwest Airlines could virtually eliminate all of their jet fuel price risk. The issue is that financial institutions are generally unwilling to offering basis swaps due to the difficulty of hedging them.

Operational Strategies

For companies that produce commodities, the operational financial risk strategies are basically what they are in business to manage and to profit from. For those corporations that use commodities as inputs, there are relatively few operational strategies for financial risk management.

The most basic operational strategy is to enter into long-term fixed price contracts from suppliers. This of course is shifting the price risk to suppliers who may or may not be willing to accept that risk. Another strategy is to pass any price risk onto customers, but this comes with its own set of associated risks. Airlines of course tried to pass commodity price risk to consumers with fuel cost surcharges on its flights during the last time that oil prices spiked. This led to significant competitive advantage for those airlines like Southwest that had mitigated their fuel price risk. It also led to customer backlash as airlines teased customers with very low flight fares, but then surprised them with high fuel surcharges. The situation got so much out of control that in Canada the government enacted legislation that forced airlines to only promote all-in fare prices in their advertising.

One of the blunt mechanisms to manage commodity price risk is to backward integrate by setting up (or purchasing) a commodity producer. This of course is what many of the fully integrated oil companies do with both upstream and downstream oil sourcing, refining, and marketing capabilities. Of course, it is also what Henry Ford so famously did with his River Rouge combined steel mill, electric generation facility, and automobile factory.

As with other blunt operational strategies, vertical integration solely for the cause of commodity price risk is probably not a sound idea. However, if the commodity is key, and if financial contracts are not sufficient to control the price risk to an acceptable degree, then the company may be left with few alternatives.

Risk Management with Derivatives

Financial derivatives are available for a wide variety of commodities. Due to the nature of commodities, most of the trading is done on the exchanges or with specialist counterparties in the over-the-counter market. Financial institutions, with some notable exceptions, are not that heavily involved in the commodity markets and particularly not for physically settled contracts. Thus, the number of counterparties for over-the-counter bespoke transactions is somewhat limited for many commodity-type derivatives. Thus, the importance of exchange traded derivatives for commodities is much greater.

Having said that, there is an opportunity to take advantage of some of the special characteristics of commodity price trends in offering exotic derivative types. These exotic derivatives are generally cash settled and mainly offered in the over-the-counter derivatives market.

One special type of exotic option that is used in commodity markets is a barrier option. A barrier option is like a conventional option in that it still offers a payout based on the price level relative to a strike price. The difference with barrier options is that there is also a barrier level in addition to the strike price. If the barrier price level is broken through by the price level of the underlying commodity, then the option either gets "knocked-out" or "knocked-in." In a knock-out option, the option is immediately canceled, and effectively ceases to exist without any payoff if the price barrier is breached. With a knock-in option, the option does not exist, and thus will not make a payout unless the barrier price is broken through.

Let's examine an example. Assume that a cereal producer is interested in hedging against the price of corn rising, and a corn farmer is interested in hedging against the price of corn falling. Both of them could buy an option on corn with a strike price of $3.50 per bushel. The cereal producer could buy a call option and the farmer could buy a put option. Assume that the current price of corn is around $3.50 per bushel, and thus both of the hedgers have bought at-the-money options which tend to be relatively expensive. Both the cereal producer and the farmer would like to reduce the cost of their hedges. Both also believe that corn prices tend to trend, that is, once they start moving in a given direction then they will continue in that direction for some period of time. That being the case, both of them can reduce the cost of their options by choosing to enter into barrier options which are less expensive than conventional options.

The cereal producer believes that if the price of corn falls to $3.00 per bushel that it is unlikely that they will need their call option. Thus, the cereal producer buys a knock-out call option on corn with a strike price of $3.50 and a knock-out barrier of $3.00. If the price of corn stays above $3.00, then the option will behave, and have a payout just like a conventional option. However, if the price of corn falls below $3.00, then the option will get "knocked-out" and cease to exist. The payout will be zero, even if the price of corn recovers and soars above the strike price of $3.50.

The farmer will likewise buy a barrier option, but they decide to buy a knock-in put option with a knock-in barrier of $3.00. In this case, the option does not exist until the price of corn falls below the barrier price of $3.00. Once the price of corn does that, then the barrier option acts exactly the same as a conventional put option.

Barrier options are popular for commodities (and sometimes for currencies) because of the tendency for commodity prices to trend. However, there is a danger of being whipsawed. For instance, in the example above, the price of corn could fall below $3.00, knocking out the cereal producer's option, and then subsequently the price of corn could soar to well over the original strike price of $3.50 and the cereal producer would be left fully exposed to corn prices. Generally, to protect against being whipsawed, hedgers will buy another option once one has been knocked out. However, if corn prices do fall below $3.00, then the cost of a call option with a strike price of $3.50 will be much less expensive than it was originally because of the new lower price of corn.

Prudently handled, barrier options provide an effective and low-cost derivative hedging tactic for certain commodities whose price changes have a tendency to trend.

Weather Derivatives

Weather derivatives are a relatively new financial markets innovation, where contract payouts are linked to measurements of weather variables. The particular variables range from temperatures, to wind speeds, to the number of days of precipitation at a particular location. Really, any measurable weather variable can be used in these contracts. Let us explore the specific example of a heating degree day (HDD) swap to help understand the concept. Although the actual calculation is a little more complicated, HDDs are, at their essence, a measurement of how cold a location is—the higher the number of HDDs, the colder a location is. Two companies could enter a swap contract where each month the fixed price payer will pay an amount equal to $1,000 multiplied by 500 and the floating price payer will pay $1,000 multiplied by the actual number of HDDs in New York. The $1,000 could be any number based on how small or large the companies want the contract to be. Here, 500 is roughly the monthly average of HDD in New York State, and would be agreed to by the companies as part of their negotiations. If the actual number of HDDs in a month is 600, the fixed price payer pays $500,000 ($1,000 × 500) and the floating price payer pays $600,000 ($1,000 × 600). In practice, only the net difference between the fixed and floating payments would change hands, so the floating price payer would make a payment of $100,000 to the fixed price payer. If the actual number of HDDs in the month is 400, the fixed price payer will make a net payment of $100,000 to the floating price payer.

The question is who would be interested in entering into a weather derivative like this? If you are a gas distribution company, your profits tend to be very highly correlated to the amount of natural gas you sell to your customers, and they tend to buy a lot more gas when it is cold as it takes more energy for them to heat their homes and businesses. In this case, the company may be worried that if a winter is unusually warm, their sales and therefore their profits will be below expectations. They will look to enter a contract where they benefit if winter temperatures are warm (i.e., there is a lower number of HDDs) to hedge their risk of lower sales and profits. By entering into an HDD swap as the floating price payer, if temperatures are warmer than normal, they receive a net payment from the floating price payer and if temperatures are lower than normal, they will make a net payment to the floating price payer. The company has reduced its exposure to variable temperatures, helping reduce volatility in its earnings.

Energy companies are natural market participants in weather derivatives since energy usage for certain sectors is so closely tied to weather. As renewable energy generation continues to increase, there will be more interest in weather derivatives tied to the amount of sunshine so solar producers can hedge their generation output, or average wind speed so wind producers can similarly hedge their output. Beyond energy companies, who else might be interested in weather derivatives? Revenue at a ski resort is likely to be significantly impacted by the amount of snow—people tend to prefer the white stuff to skiing on grass and rocks. As the resort owner, you could pray to a divine being for snowfall, or you could enter into a weather derivative that pays you if snowfall is below normal to mitigate the impact of lost revenues in a snowless winter. The following Corney & Barrow case study describes one quirky example of a corporation using weather derivatives to hedge their operating revenues.

Case Study

Corney & Barrow

Corney & Barrow as part of their business own a chain of wine bars in London, and in 2000 entered into a weather derivatives contract. At first blush, you may not think of bars as natural market participants in the world of weather derivatives, but there is an undeniable logic to their thought process. At six of Corney & Barrow's locations, there were outdoor seating areas, and fully one-fifth of their summer profits were attributable to customers who came out to enjoy London's fleeting warm sunny days. A cool dreary summer would reduce Corney & Barrow's profits; so to hedge this risk they entered a contract that would see them receive payments up to £15,000 on each Thursday and Friday between June and September when temperatures failed to reach 24° C (75°F) to a maximum of £100,000 over the course of the summer. The contract was option-like in that Corney & Barrow would make a fixed payment regard-less of the weather outcome, receive a payment if the summer was cool, but not make a further payment if temperatures were warm. They were effectively buying an option contract to protect them from one side of the risk equation (lower profits driven by cool weather) while fully benefiting, less the fixed payment, from higher revenues if it turned out to be a warm summer. Other contracts (cooling degree day or temperature swaps, for example) could have been used to eliminate exposure to both higher and lower temperatures. Interestingly, the party on the other end of Corney & Barrow's contract was Enron, a major energy company that was confident in its ability to integrate the contract into its broad portfolio.[4]

Concluding Thoughts

Commodity price risk has some unique characteristics that also create unique challenges for managing it. The main characteristic of commodities is their physical nature. A large number of trading in commodities are done by producers of the commodities or users of the commodities. In the other areas of financial risk that we have discussed, there are a large number of traders who are trading for speculative gain—that is not as much the case for commodities. The physical nature also means that basis risk is more important, as differences in quality of the underlying, transportation of the underlying, or geographical location of the underlying can make a significant difference in value. It is a lot easier to trade exchange rates digitally than it is to deal with a trainload of corn.

Despite the challenges in managing commodity price risk, it is important to remember that as long as consumers buy physical assets, commodity risk management will be a very important part of business risk management.

---

[4]The Economist. June 15, 2000. "Buying a Financial Umbrella." http://www.economist.com/node/82532

CHAPTER 10

Financial Risk Management Governance

Introduction

By now it should be clear that proper financial risk management can add significant value to an organization. However, like most things of great usefulness, it needs proper governance or oversight. When financial risk management first became prevalent in the early 1990's, the proper level of governance was often lacking. As a result, there were several prominent risk management debacles. In large part, the debacles were caused by derivatives. However, derivatives are simply tools for financial risk management; whether that risk management is for speculative purposes or for supporting the objectives of a nonfinancial firm. The problem was not derivatives, but governance. The financial crisis of 2008 was also in large part brought about through the lack of governance, but this time the lack of governance was on a systemic scale. The lack of governance in the use of derivatives led famed investor Warren Buffett to famously remark that derivatives are "weapons of financial mass destruction."

Case Study
Procter and Gamble

Procter and Gamble is a large company known to most, but even for those not familiar with the company name, virtually everyone will be familiar with many of the consumer products they sell around the world: Crest toothpaste, Bounty paper towel, and Gillette razors to name just a few. Clearly P&G are masters of consumer products, but what became equally clear in 1994 was that their interest rate risk management was not at the same level. In April 1994, P&G disclosed that they had lost $157 million on interest rate derivatives. Although relatively small when compared with some other hedging- and derivatives-related disasters, this episode is highly instructive on a number of fronts. The losses arose from two swap contracts they had entered with Bankers Trust. One contract saw P&G pay a fixed rate and receive a floating rate that would vary inversely to U.S. interest rates. The other contract was similar, but tied to German interest rates instead of U.S. rates. Simply put, P&G would benefit if interest rates stayed flat or fell and would lose if interest rates rose. The complex formula in these contracts effectively created substantial leverage, which would see P&G's payment rise much faster than general interest rates. Unfortunately for P&G, as you have probably already guessed, interest rates began to rise, and P&G's borrowing rates reportedly soared to an incredible 14.12 percent above the general commercial paper rates.[1]

P&G sued Bankers Trust and reached a settlement which was that Bankers Trust forgo most of the money owed to them by P&G, but how did they end up in that situation to begin with? Although interest rate derivatives to convert fixed rate payments to variable rates can be part of a normal corporate hedging program, these transactions and their asymmetric risk profiles did not appear to be effective hedges for P&G. These transactions were not really hedges at all, but speculation on the direction of interest rates with the objective of profit generation to lower total borrowing costs. In its 1994 10-K filing, P&G referred to these contracts as "out of policy" and that "At June 30, 1994, no such instruments were in our portfolio and it is the Company's intent not to enter such leveraged contracts in the future."[2] This demonstrates the importance of having a well-structured policy with appropriate governance and controls to ensure that the policy is being followed. P&G also believed that they were taken advantage of by Bankers Trust, and given the settlement, this may not be untrue. It should also be noted that Bankers Trust was accused by a

---

[1]S. Hansell. October, 1994. "P.& G. Sues Bankers Trust Over Swap Deal." http://www.nytimes.com/1994/10/28/business/p-g-sues-bankers-trust-over-swap-deal.html
[2]U.S. Securities and Exchange Commission. https://www.sec.gov/Archives/edgar/data/80424/0000080424-94-000021.txt

number of other companies of similar unscrupulous sales tactics, reaching settlements with other companies and the SEC. However, ensuring that employees who are responsible for entering these transactions have the knowledge and experience to understand the products being offered is a common-sense approach to mitigating the risk. A simple rule of thumb is that if you don't understand the product being offered and the risks that it entails, it shouldn't be purchased!

We do not take such a dim view of financial risk management, nor the use of the derivatives. Properly governed, financial risk management and the use of derivatives are not only safe and practical, but also necessary if a firm wants to be competitive. In fact, we believe that not harnessing the usefulness of financial risk management, and implementing the full range of risk management strategies, including derivatives, is imprudent and indeed reckless. However, implementing financial risk management without proper governance is equally imprudent and reckless.

In this chapter, we will go through the basic governance guidelines for effective financial risk management. Included is a special section intended for those in positions of leadership such as senior managers and the Board. The steps for good governance are not complicated, and for the most part are straightforward common sense. The main problem seems to be that few companies, and few managers, and in particular few Board members are willing to take the time to learn a few basic principles of risk management—a problem that this book was written to correct.

Risk management is now often incorrectly assumed to be too complex and too specialized for the generalist to understand. This leads to risk management being left to the experts and this is the beginning of virtually all of the problems that we encounter in financial risk management. Compounding the issue is that the assumption that risk management is best left to the experts means that those whose role is governance—namely senior managers and Board members—are reluctant to ask the necessary questions when they should for fear of being exposed as unknowledgeable, or even worse stupid and ill-suited for their position. This is fundamentally an issue of organizational self-esteem and in our opinion is the ultimate cancer for effective financial risk management and risk management governance. We will discuss this point at more length later in this chapter.

Basic Necessities for Risk Management Governance

There are four basic necessities for effective risk management governance. They are: (i) develop and communicate the financial risk management philosophy, (ii) have measureable financial risk management objectives, (iii) have a data management system that ensures that the risk management objectives are being met, and (iv) clear lines of control, accountability, and limits.

Develop and Communicate the Financial Risk Management Philosophy

The first necessity for risk management governance and for effective risk management is to have a sound philosophy guiding the risk management practices of the firm. This seems to be so obvious as to not merit mention, yet in our experience few companies have a financial risk management philosophy.

Organizations exist to accomplish tasks, and to accomplish tasks involve risk. Those risks may be good risks or they may be negative risks. They may be financial risks or they may be strategic or operational risks. The risk management philosophy is a basic statement of what risks the organization exists for and what magnitude of those risks it is willing to take. Business organizations exist to take business risks of developing and marketing products and services. Not-for-profit organizations exist to develop a necessary product or service or to promote a cause. Public sector entities exist to provide services to their constituents. Each of these activities involves a portfolio of risks and thus all types of organizations exist to manage risk in some shape or form.

The financial risk management philosophy may or may not be separate from the firm's overall risk management philosophy—particularly if the organization has embraced enterprise risk management. The risk management philosophy basically states what risks the organization is in business to take, or to manage. Secondly, it states how much risk the organization is willing to take to achieve its goals. Finally, and perhaps implicitly, it states the risks that are not central to the firm's existence. A firm, for example, may decide to eliminate interest rate risk, mitigate currency risk, and embrace commodity risk. The issue is whether the choice of risks and the degree of acceptable risk are consciously taken, consistently stated, and properly managed, understood, and communicated to all relevant stakeholders.

As an example of the importance of choosing a risk philosophy, consider the simple example of gold mining companies. See, for example, the case study of Barrick Gold in Chapter 9. Gold mining companies tend to fall into two very distinct types. There are those gold mining companies who do not hedge gold prices. These are companies that essentially state that their risk philosophy is that they are a gold-risk-loving company. These companies are essentially in business to capture gold price risk. By contrast, there are other gold mining companies that hedge most, if not all, of their anticipated gold production against fluctuating gold prices. These gold companies are not in business to take on gold price risk. It is a very sharp difference in financial risk management philosophy. Stakeholders, and in particular equity shareholders, can select which type of gold mining company they would want to invest in. A gold mining company that does not hedge production is a company that you would invest in if you want to have exposure to gold prices. A gold mining company that hedges gold price risk extensively is a mining company that you would invest in if you think they are going to be more efficient at mining than their peers.

A second illustration of the principle of risk philosophy is multinational companies that are U.S. based. Some of these companies hedge virtually all of their currency exposure while some make it a point to not hedge their currency exposure. Those companies that do not hedge their currency exposure are seen as useful diversification investments against a slumping U.S. economy, while those that hedge their currency exposures are viewed as pure plays on the products or services that they offer. In this context, we have heard Chief Financial Officers claim, "our shareholders want and expect us to hedge all financial risks that are not central to our operations," and we have also heard different Chief Financial Officers claim, "our shareholders do not want or expect us to hedge." It is not a case of one Chief Financial Officer being correct and the other being incorrect. What it does point out is that risk management starts with knowing what the risk management philosophy of the firm is and that there are a variety of forms that an organization's risk philosophy can take.

After deciding which financial risks are key to the firm's operations, and which are not, the next step of the financial risk philosophy is to determine the level of risk that is acceptable or desired. For some financial risks, the amount of tolerable risk may be very high, while for others the amount of tolerable risk will be very low. A general rule of thumb is that the greater the operational and strategic risk, then the lower the financial risk should be. This rule of course assumes that financial risk is not central to the operations of the organization, such as it would be for a gold mining company that consciously chooses to accept (embrace?) gold price risk.

Setting the financial risk management philosophy is a key function of the Board. Ultimately, the risk philosophy should be set by the shareholders of the firm (although other stakeholders will certainly have an opinion), and thus the Board is the proper place for the financial risk philosophy to be set. Governance in its most basic form sees to it that the philosophy is set, communicated, and followed. The following Florida Electric Utilities Case Study shows the confusion that can follow from a poorly communicated risk management philosophy.

Case Study
Florida Electric Utilities

In the summer of 2015, media reports began circulating about losses of over $6 billion incurred by Florida's electric utilities resulting from natural gas hedges from 2002 to 2015. Natural gas prices in Florida tend to track Henry Hub, which allows the liquid futures and options market at this hub to be effective hedge for consumers in Florida. Natural gas prices reached peaks in 2005 and 2008 as supply disruptions from hurricanes and other factors pushed prices to between $10 and $15/MMBtu, but then as the shale boom occurred and U.S. natural gas production grew too fast for demand to keep up, prices trended lower, falling under $2/MMBtu on several occasions. At the time, Florida's utilities were shifting their generation away from coal and oil toward natural gas. To hedge exposure to natural gas pricing, these utilities purchased futures contracts or entered into fixed price contracts for their natural gas supply.

If prices had risen, these contracts would have benefited customers, but as prices fell they instead created losses. These losses meant that utilities, and their customers, did not fully benefit from the cheaper natural gas available in the open market; in this case, customers would have been better off by more than $6 billion had these utilities not hedged their natural gas during this period. The four main investor-owned electric utilities in Florida proposed in early 2016 to reduce their hedging by 25 percent; however, in November 2016, they filed with the regulator for a complete moratorium on new hedges through the end of 2017.

This saga raises several important issues that much be addressed in designing and implementing any hedging strategy. Firstly, what is the objective of the program? Is it to reduce or eliminate as much volatility as possible, to protect against significant movements in only one direction, something else more specific to a company's underlying financial performance, or a combination of several objectives? Secondly, what are the key risks related to the program and what are the implications if something doesn't go as planned? Lastly, are all relevant stakeholders sufficiently informed about hedging in general, and about the specific objectives and risks of the hedging plan being implemented? In this case, the utilities working together with customer representatives and the regulator to reach consensus on an appropriate approach to hedging that is well understood and meets the needs of all stakeholders could help to avoid future situations like this. It must be noted that hedging programs will often look worst at times when it is best to hedge, in this case after significant declines in prices, perhaps there is now limited downside left and risk is skewed to the upside. Markets tend to be cyclical, and evaluation of the success of a hedging program must be done for at least a full market cycle, and ideally over several complete cycles.

Have Measureable Financial Risk Management Objectives

A closely related step to the risk philosophy is the risk management objective. The objective is simply the answer to the question "what is the risk management function supposed to do?" Is it to eliminate risk? Is it to keep risk within certain bounds? Is it to increase the value of the firm through prudent risk management?

One method for setting the objective is to develop a listing of the various financial risk exposures that the organization has, or potentially could have, and a guideline to the level of acceptance that it has for each of the risks. You will recall from Chapter 2 that there are a range of responses that a firm may take to risk. The range we suggested was: eliminate, avoid, mitigate, ignore, embellish, and embrace. The key is to develop the list and then have clearly defined responses to each of the risks. The definitions of the range of responses should, if possible, be defined in terms of quantitative exposures, and preferably in monetary values of the risk exposure that were listed in Chapter 4. One of the advantages of financial risk management (as opposed to, for example, strategic or operational risk) is that financial risks are almost always capable of being quantitatively assessed. In setting the financial risk management objective, this ability to quantify risk exposures should be exploited.

The setting of the financial risk management objective should allow the organization to produce clear answers to the following questions: is the organization's financial risk management effective, and is the risk management function achieving the objectives set out for it? It is surprising considering the number of companies that cannot answer these very basic questions, yet still keep expanding their financial risk management operations without being able to answer the basic question of whether or not the risk management function is doing a decent job.

We believe that the ideal is to be able to quantify the amount of value that the risk management function is adding to the firm. Conceptually this is ideal, but it also has some possible unintended consequences. In the past, many firms interpreted this to be making the Treasury function a profit center through the use of aggressive financing strategies using derivative tactics that they were not sophisticated enough to fully understand and monitor. This was the case with the well-known debacle of Procter and Gamble, which used sophisticated interest rate swaps as part of their financing strategy.

A second issue of quantifying the use of financial risk management is that a risk avoided generally never gets considered or factored into the analysis, when in reality the risk avoided may be the most important analysis of all. For instance, if the risk management function actions prevent a loss in foreign sales due to adverse currency moves, then it may be the case that it is assumed that it was the marketing function that did a great job, rather than the risk function whose actions prevented necessary price increases to keep profit margins at the same level. Note that the risk function may add value through avoiding a negative risk as in the previous example or it may destroy value through preventing the organization from seizing an opportunity due to positive risk. For instance, without any hedging, the currency rate could have moved in the organization's favor allowing them to increase market share or increase profits. These negative actions should also be counted when assessing whether or not the risk management function is adding value. In considering this, the reader may want to think back to the discussion about using option versus forward type strategies that were discussed in Chapter 4. It is quite possible for risk management actions to destroy value beyond the explicit cost of risk management through its effect on operations or strategy.

One method to calculate the value of the risk management function is to do a Monte Carlo type analysis of the actions for the firm both with and without risk management actions. By examining the two distributions produced, it should be clear of the value that the risk management function is producing. Obviously building a Monte Carlo analysis for the firm is a difficult task. However, doing so strikes at the heart of understanding what the factors are that are driving the success of the firm, as well as how well managers understand them.

If it is not possible to build an overall Monte Carlo model for the firm, then at a minimum the firm ought to be able to build a rudimentary model for each division. While a divisional model will overlook the synergies and correlations of the actions across the firm, it will at least capture the main points. The goal here is not perfection in the model, but developing an idea of what risk management tactics are likely to be more effective. Even a very simple Monte Carlo model will generate valuable discussions about not only the risk management function, but also the overall management of the firm.

Have a Data Management System to Ensure the Above Issues Are Being Satisfied

In order to accomplish the task of assessing whether the risk management function is doing an adequate job, it is necessary to have data systems in place to capture and disseminate the appropriate metrics. Does the organization have accurate and readily available (and understandable) reports that allow senior managers and Directors to answer the questions of if the financial risk management function is being effective and if the lines of control and accountability are being respected and within preset limits.

The goal here is not to measure everything, nor is it to measure everything to a high degree of accuracy. Neither is it to have perfect forecasting. It is our belief that too much emphasis has been placed on the quantitative analysis without enough consideration of what should be analyzed. An old adage of risk management is that it is far better to be approximately right than to be precisely wrong.

A key element of the data management system is that it be timely, and that it be accessible. It is of little to no use to have data that is highly accurate, yet out of date by the time it is available for use by the managers who can take action based on what the data is telling them. Likewise, data analysis that is only understandable to a select few is also of little to no use. Thus, a key element of a data management system is to develop a risk dashboard that is timely, focused on the key elements or risks that the firm must manage, and in an easily readable and understandable form.

The risk dashboard should be just like the risk dashboard on your car. It should be easy to read, providing timely data feedback, have only the key variables that you need to read, and have warning lights, such as your check engine light, that activate when unusual activity requiring action or further investigation is necessary. In addition, the risk dashboard should tie directly back to the objectives of the risk management function.

Many organizations, particularly financial institutions, issue what is commonly known as a 4:15 report. This report is issued daily and generally has as its key feature the Value at Risk for the day of the firm. It is issued at such a time so that action, if necessary, may be taken by senior managers before it is too late in the day. It is a brief report, and in ideal circumstances can be read, and understood, in an instant.

The mere exercise of developing an effective risk dashboard is useful in and of itself. By developing a risk dashboard, the organization is forced to think about what is really important and critical about its risk management functions. It is likely that the initial development will produce changes in setting the risk philosophy, the financial risk management objectives, and in how the data is collected and processed.

Have Clear Lines of Control, Accountability, and Limits

With the risk philosophy, the risk management objectives, and the data systems in place, it is necessary to implement and put the risk management strategy into action. To do so, there need to be clear lines of control, accountability, and limits.

The first issue is to have lines of control, with checks and counterchecks. Many of the risk debacles are caused by an initial mistake being made by a risk manager or a trader charged with implementing a risk management strategy. Since in most of these cases there is no clear line of control or countercheck, the manager naturally tries to first cover up the mistake and then secondly to attempt to fix the mistake. The issue becomes that the cover-up and the attempt to fix (still without admitting that there is an issue) cause more complicated and complex issues than the initial error.

Depending on the level of sophistication of the risk management strategies employed, it is likely that the person implementing the risk strategy will not be the one deciding on what the risk strategy should be. The key issue is that there need to be methods to ensure that the risk management strategy is being properly implemented. This is a communication issue. Managers of the staff doing the implementation have to be knowledgeable enough to be able to check that the strategy is properly implemented. Secondly, they need to allow for questions to go both ways so that there are no misunderstandings in terms of the intentions of the risk plan. Thirdly, the data systems need to be robust so that unintended actions cannot be taken, and if such actions are taken that they are flagged. Again, too often, the data management system is controlled by those doing the implementation. This leads to potential for them to adjust the data feeds going to management in such a way as to paint an overly optimistic and misleading picture. The data management system is a key communication tool in making sure that the right data is getting to, and being understood by the right managers.

The third broad element needed is a proper set of limits. There should be limits, coupled with well-defined policies, on who can do what in terms of risk management, how much of it they can do, and in the case of derivatives where, and with whom they can conduct trades with. The time to do due diligence on trading activities is before activities are undertaken; not after a risk debacle has occurred.

Most companies with a sophisticated risk management function delineate implementing the risk management strategy into three separate functions or offices. The "front office" is where the risk management strategies are actually implemented. The front office is where the derivative trades are done, and where the specific tactics are chosen. The "middle office" does the calculation of the exposures, both the risk exposures of the firm, as well as the exposures of the risk management strategies. The middle office will keep track of the size of the risk manager's positions, and also keeps track of related data such as the level of counterparty exposure to each of the firm's counterparties. Finally, the middle office is generally responsible for ensuring that limits are respected and for escalating to senior managers in case of risk management activities beyond preset boundaries. The third leg, the "back office" takes care of the nitty-gritty operational details such as making sure that the proper cash flows are being received and sent for any contracts entered into. The back office also checks that the contracts and paperwork are properly executed, recorded, and in line with the risk strategy. This three-pronged separation of duties creates a robust set of checks and balances and allows for issues to quickly come to light.

Case Study
Barings Bank

Barings Bank was founded in 1762 and operated for nearly 250 years before unauthorized trading losses of more than $1 billion saw the bank collapse and be purchased by Dutch bank ING for £1. This debacle, which has been made into a movie, *Rogue Trader*, highlights key operational and governance risks and the devastating impact that can result if these risks are not properly managed.

Nick Leeson, a 28-year-old Brit, was working as a trader in Baring's Singapore office, where he executed trades on behalf of the Bank's clients, and looked to capitalize on arbitrage opportunities in Asian financial markets. Leeson had been very successful for several years, generating profits of £10 million in 1993, 10 percent of the bank's total earnings. A trading error resulted in losses for the firm, but Leeson didn't want to admit the error to head office, and felt that he would be able to earn the money back before it was detected. Things did not go according to plan and the losses compounded. In an attempt to make up the larger shortfall, Leeson kept increasing the size of his bets, risking more and more of Barings' capital. He was also able to open a new account, the now infamous "88888" account in which he buried the losses, helping avoid detection from head office. At one point, Leeson had wagered $29 billion in equities, currencies, and interest rates, and losses ended up exceeding $1 billion.[3] Eventually these losses were discovered, and Leeson was arrested in Germany after fleeing Singapore. He ended up being sentenced to 6½ years in prison.[4]

What were the key risk management failings that led to this debacle? Leeson was effectively running the front office (trading) side, the middle office (risk exposure measurement) side, and the back office (settlements and accounting) side of the Singapore office. This structure allowed him to create the 88888 account and falsify reports and documentation. The three-tiered control structure of a front, middle, and back office was not present. Lesson was responsible for both making trades, as well as verifying the exposure and limits on those trades. Additionally, he was responsible for maintaining the paperwork for his activities. Thus, Lesson was a single person controlling both trade execution and trade settlement, which allowed him to hide losses until they got out of control. In addition, the overall governance structure at Barings was deficient. The fact that a 20-something-year-old trader in a remote location thousands of miles from head office was able to enter these trades without

---

[3] R.W. Stevenson. February, 1995. "The Collapse of Barings: The Overview; Young Trader's $29 Billion Bet Brings Down a Venerable Firm." http://www.nytimes.com/1995/02/28/us/collapse-barings-overview-young-trader-s-29-billion-bet-brings-down-venerable.html?pagewanted=all

[4] J. Rodrigues. February, 2015. "Barings Collapse at 20: How Rogue Trader Nick Leeson Broke the Bank" https://www.theguardian.com/business/from-the-archive-blog/2015/feb/24/nick-leeson-barings-bank-1995-20-archive

full knowledge of senior leadership at the bank, and that he was able to continue receiving additional funding to support these trades shows that oversight was severely lacking. It appears that few senior managers had enough experience, knowledge, or self-esteem to ask what was going on. The Board and senior managers appeared willing to turn a blind eye until it was simply no longer possible for them to do so; but by then it was too late for Barings.

Other Elements of Effective Governance

Risk management is implemented by people, and thus ultimately the quality of risk management in an organization is the quality of the personnel implementing risk management. Hiring talent is an art, and for risk management in particular. The focus on risk management certifications has led to a number of individuals becoming very knowledgeable about risk, but we believe that being a competent risk manager goes well beyond knowledge. Risk management requires not only knowledge but also creativity and intuition—both skills that are very difficult to learn through a book or a course. Risk management is a skill that is developed by being curious, by being willing to think, by developing creative stories about possibilities for the future, and by learning through experience.

Historically, risk managers were experienced managers who had "been there and done that." However, with the increase in sophisticated techniques, the trend has been for those with education over experience. The sweet spot though is likely in the middle; having a proper combination of experience and training. Given that, training is a key component of risk management, and not solely for those who will be risk managers themselves. While financial risk management, as opposed to the more generalized enterprise risk management, is admittedly more of a discipline for a specialist, the reality is that risk management should be a part of everyone's responsibility. For instance, frontline managers can often sense a chance in market conditions, well before sophisticated traders in front of their data screens can. It is this institutional participation in risk thinking from varied parts of the organization that is so valuable to harvest.

Given that, training thus becomes a key component of having best-in-class risk management. Training helps to increase awareness of risk management issues, and illustrates the importance of risk management for competitive advantage. Training also creates a common language and set of assumptions around risk management, which significantly improves implementation of the risk management strategy. With training, the entire organization has the potential to become the eyes and ears of the organization in terms of risk; a better data set cannot be purchased. Perhaps most importantly, training increases acceptance of the risk management objectives. When employees understand risk practices, and when they are given the understanding and rationale for such practices, they will be much more accepting and compliant. They will also become much more willing to proactively integrate the risk management department in designing new corporate initiatives.

Risk training is also essential for senior managers and Directors. Senior managers and Directors need the risk training so that they can ask quality questions about the risk management plan and implementation and respond appropriately to the answers provided. They are not necessarily going to become risk managers themselves, but good corporate governance and good risk governance demand that they be able to carry on the necessary discussions surrounding risk management issues with those who are responsible for implementing the risk management plan. Virtually all risk management debacles are caused in part when the risk management team knows that they can act with impunity due to ignorance of those who are supposed to be supervising them.

Ultimately, the responsibility for risk management belongs with the Board. If the Board cannot carry out that responsibility effectively, then the corporation will be exposed. Risk management training is essential to ensure this is not the case.

Another component of good risk management is that appropriate and ongoing investment be made in the risk management function and implementation. Often, risk management is seen as a burdensome cost center. Seeing risk management as a center in which sufficient investment should be made yields significant dividends. As implied throughout this book, risk management is not a nice to have, but instead is a must have. Admittedly, there will be different needs and different scopes of necessary risk management operations needed for different firms based on their activities. However, it is difficult to conceive of an organization that cannot benefit from a suitable investment in risk management. The issue is that risk management is often considered as an afterthought, not as a central factor in success. That is a mistake in our opinion.

Part of the necessary investment in risk management is an ongoing review of policies and practices. Risk is an evolving field, both in its practice, and because of the new risks that are constantly arising in the global marketplace. Good risk management governance implies that the organization will respond to the evolving risk landscape with continual updating and renewal and training. Financial risk management is not a one-time implementation. It needs to be constantly reset and refreshed to be effective. The risk philosophy, the objectives of the financial risk management function, the controls and limits, the risk metrics, and the lines of accountability all need to be reexamined on a regular basis.

Of course, as stated earlier, the effectiveness of the risk management function needs to be continually examined as well. The organization needs to check on what lessons it is learning from its experience with risk management. Risk is a learning activity and the firm should not only be tracking its risk management results to determine its effectiveness, but also for the lessons it can be learning.

A final component to effective risk governance is to create a positive culture around risk management. A positive culture around risk management has several components. It is part of a function of training, so the organization's staff understands what they should be doing in terms of risk management and why they are doing it.

A second component to a healthy risk culture is to have an appropriate emphasis on risk management so as to ensure the risk function, policies, and procedures are appropriate to the activities of the firm and not choking off normal activity. Risk management should be enabling the business rather than being seen as a bureaucratic burden halting progress. Risk management should be seen as a friend or helpful ally to the business lines. Risk should never be seen as "The Department of No!"

A third component to creating a positive risk culture is counterintuitive; namely, to allow mistakes. If staff are allowed to make mistakes, then not only will they be encouraged to learn from their mistakes, but they will be more willing to bring mistakes forward so they can be acted upon, rather than hidden as in the Nick Leeson experience at Barings Bank. Risk management is not effective if it operates in a culture of fear. Risk management explicitly recognizes that bad and good things can happen and will happen. Risk is not a fool-proof science. Mistakes will happen, but overly severe consequences for mistakes only create a host of unintended negative consequences.

A positive risk culture is ultimately the sign of healthy risk governance. It implies that the firm has risk appropriately embedded into the culture and the daily activities of the firm, and that risk is seen as helpful to the cause of accomplishing the strategic objectives.

Guidelines for Senior Managers and Directors

Risk management ultimately is the responsibility of senior managers and the Board. In particular, the Board sets the tone and owns responsibility for risk governance. While it is not their responsibility to dwell on the specifics, the Board needs to be responsible for having robust discussions surrounding the setting of the financial risk philosophy and the objective of the financial risk management objectives. In particular, the Board needs to agree with and approve management's recommendations for the responses to each of the financial risks.

To adequately fulfill their obligations, Board members need to stay abreast of risk management developments, both within and beyond the boundaries of the organization. They need to ensure that they get the proper education so they can properly assess the risk strategy.

The specifics of the Board in fulfilling their obligations is in asking the appropriate questions and just as importantly being able to understand and critically examine the answers that are forthcoming. As mentioned in the previous section, risk management troubles tend to start when the risk management function believes that those responsible for oversight, namely, the senior management team and the Board, do not have the will to gain the necessary knowledge and understanding they need to provide adequate oversight. To provide good risk governance, the Board needs to question risk assumptions, question risk tactics, and question risk results.

In Chapter 3, we put forward some essential risk questions, namely, what can happen, when can it happen, and how much of an effect can it have? These questions are an excellent starting point for the Board to begin its risk management discussions at a meeting.

The final component for Board members to remember is that risk is forward looking. Most experienced Board members are naturally very good at this; that is how they got to be Board members in the first place. Much risk analysis and Board reports that we have seen are focused on what has happened, not what might happen. What has happened is interesting for the lessons that can be learned, but beyond that the past is not a good way to plan for the future. Risk evolves, and the organization's risk practices need to evolve as well to meet the future, not to be great for a past that is likely never to reoccur.

Ultimately, Board members got to be Board members because of their business intuition. In our view, business intuition is also risk intuition. Although risk management is a somewhat specialized branch of financial management, competent Board members will rely on their intuition, and that by itself will make them competent for good risk governance. The issue is when they meekly defer to the financial risk experts, who may have the risk knowledge, but not the experience that is so important. Poor Board members accept uncritically the reports they are given; great Board members keep asking questions until they are satisfied.

Concluding Thoughts

An organization can have world-class risk management ideas and systems; however, without proper risk governance, it will all be for naught. A great risk strategy and great implementation will almost always underperform a more modest risk management program that has proper governance. It is our belief that risk governance is the central role of the senior management team and the Board. Financial risk management is a key part of the overall risk governance.

CHAPTER 11

The Future of Financial Risk Management

Predicting the future has always been a task fraught with risk. However, we will take the risk and put forward a few comments to conclude.

Risk management has always been an evolving field, but it seems that financial risk management is on the cusp of some potentially revolutionary changes. There are structural issues for financial risk management, technological issues, and finally issues that relate financial risk management to one's corporate career.

Structural Issues for FRM

At the beginning of this book we mentioned some of the structural issues that are making financial risk management so relevant. These structural issues include globalization, the rise of financial technology, or fintech as it is now popularly referred to, cybersecurity, climate change, demographics, and how geopolitical issues are changing the face of business in general. Some of these are interrelated with technology issues which we will discuss in the next section.

Conceptually globalization is the main element changing the face of risk management. Globalization involves risk management on many different fronts. The most obvious is that business is now global and thus competition is now global. No business is left isolated or unaffected by global market events. Furthermore, globalization, combined with the omniscience of social media means that global events spread virtually instantaneously, and also literally spread in a virtual fashion. Events can, and are, lived vicariously and instantaneously via social media. Consumer shopping is now a virtual and global experience. Price risk is now also global and virtual, but the effects are real.

Globalization not only means the spread of competitors is greater, it also means that the competitors can have different strategies, different backgrounds, different business models, and different approaches and perceptions of risk. No longer are companies acting in a sea of similar characters. They now have to react to actors from different cultures.

The perception of risk aspect cannot be underrated. Risk perception differs between cultures but also differs between generations. For example, today's stock market investors, and the conceptual collective that Boards are acting on behalf of, perceive investment risk very differently than investors did just a generation ago. Market risk premiums, the premium expected return for investing in risky assets, have been falling dramatically, and falling on a global basis. Once dividend-paying stocks were the darling of both Wall Street and Main Street, but now dividends are all but virtually forgotten. Everyone wants to talk about the stock that they bought that tripled in price within a month. No one seems to care anymore about a steady 4 percent dividend yield.

Part of the change in market risk premiums is likely due to the graying of the population. As the baby-boom generation moves into its peak retirement planning years, the available investment alternatives seem especially poor. As of late 2017, interest rates, and by extension bond yields, are at historically low levels. As baby-boomers look to place their retirement portfolios, they need to search for risk in order to get what they perceive to be acceptable absolute yields. Risk perception changes. This has significant implications for how companies position themselves in terms of business risk and financial risk. As the pressure rises for corporations to take on more business risk and financial risk in order to produce sufficient returns for investors, the need for financial risk management becomes all the greater. The margin of error is much smaller, and has more drastic consequences for being wrong than ever before.

This domestic pressure for enhanced stock price returns is multiplied by the easy availability of capital for entrepreneurs to start business disrupter companies such as Uber, or AirBnB, or Amazon. Companies in all industries are looking on with both pity and fear at industries like the newspaper industry that have been gutted by technology and novel business models.

Business risk has never been higher, but it has also probably never been as exciting. This climate of business risk though changes the dynamics for risk management. Furthermore, it is not whether risk management is more necessary than ever (it most definitely is in our opinion), but the question is if risk management is business. In other words, is risk management becoming more important of a business discipline, or is risk management just getting absorbed into the natural core of business activity without there being a distinction of it as a separate activity. Either way, the importance of possessing risk management skills increases.

Social media has also brought more complexity to risk management. You will recall from Chapter 1 that complexity arises when agents (consumers, competitors, investors, regulators, politicians, etc.) can interact, and can adapt or change their behavior or their decisions or their way of thinking. The prime example of complex situations is that we see the property of emergence. Thus stock market bubbles form and then burst; consumer fads grow and then fade away just as quickly; political movements such as Arab Spring or Brexit change the political landscape almost overnight, and so on. Managing complexity requires a different set of skills than the coldly analytical and complicated skills that are so well rewarded by university programs and certification programs, which grant degrees and certification based on correctly answering objective multiple choice questions, rather than showing wisdom gained through experience or the ability to have intuition about a situation.

This brings a demographic challenge for risk management beyond the differences in risk perceptions previously noted. In the past, risk management was for the most part staffed with experienced professionals who had the necessary experience to deal with situations. Like many industries though, risk management is dealing with a massive roll-off of experienced managers as the baby-boomers retire. The challenge is, will there be enough risk managers with the proper experience to take their place? It is a problem facing the trucking industry as well, but there is the prospect of self-driving trucks that has the potential to fill the forecasted shortfall of truck drivers. Do we want "self-driving" risk managers? Risk pioneer Felix Kloman, in a paper submitted to the 25th anniversary of The Institute of Risk Managers, predicted that risk management will be based on "sophisticated computer models, operated online will be modified by a sensible intuition born of long experience within the organization."[1] It seems that

---

[1] F. Kloman. 2011. "A Snitch in Time", Paper submitted for The Institute of Risk Management 25th Anniversary.

the sophisticated computer models aspect will be fulfilled, but what about the modification by "sensible intuition born of long experience"?

Technology Issues

Artificial intelligence, big data, real-time data, the internet of things; combined with "fintech" these elements together have the potential to dramatically change how financial risk management is managed. If it were not for the element of complexity, it really is quite possible that financial risk management could in the very near future be managed by an expert computer system. If we are wrong, and financial risk management is not as much of an art as it is a science, and it is simply a science, then the field will be quickly dominated by computers.

We do not believe that will happen. In the more basic field of investment management it has been tried again and again, with eventual failure being the consistent result. We believe in Felix Kloman's previously stated dictum, that risk management needs "modification" by smart, creative, and intuitive risk managers. However, only a fool would deny the awesome potential that the emerging confluence of technologies can bring to risk management.

Technology is changing, and will continue to change how risk is assessed and managed. But technology is also changing risk itself. We have talked about the global nature and the speed, but data, digitization, machine learning, cybersecurity, personal data issues, complications of social media, and a host of factors and unintended consequences yet to be discovered are changing the very nature of risk.

Ultimately risk management is about people. Technology is changing how we interact with others, but risk is still about people. Technology can help us observe and measure and assess risk, but we still need people to manage risk. Undeniably, technology is going to play an increasing role in risk management, and particularly so in financial risk management since it is price based. (Computers can deal much better with objective numerals such as prices, than they can with subjective human elements such as feelings and emotions.) The successful risk manager will be the one who can combine the best of technology with the best of intuition.

Role of Financial Risk Management on a Personal Basis

If we are correct that risk management is increasing in importance, then it stands to reason that being competent, indeed being competitive in risk management, is key to one's personal career progression.

Paradoxically, we see that risk management is simultaneously becoming a field of increasing specialization, and also becoming more mainstream in the corporate world. The tools and techniques required of a risk specialist are becoming ever more advanced and sophisticated. This had led to the rise of a variety of different risk manager certifications and advanced university degree programs devoted to financial risk management. While this is happening, it is also true that the general manager can no longer ignore risk, or assume it is the sole responsibility of a separate department. Risk management and risk knowledge are becoming the role of everyone.

The expectations on Board members in terms of risk management have probably been the greatest. Regulatory requirements, demands of stakeholders, and the pace of development of risk management practices and techniques have all accelerated. Board members are expected to be out in front of all of these changes; not necessarily on the specifics, but on the spirit of the changes and their potential. Increasingly, Board members are being selected for their experience and knowledge of risk management. It is no longer acceptable to be a passive Board member when the topic of risk management is brought up. Boards need to be proactive on risk, and that requires not only a knowledge of risk, but also an appreciation for the potential of risk management to be a major part of the competitive advantage of an institution.

Concluding Thoughts

Thus we come to the end of this chapter, and to the end of this book. As risk practitioners, we are very energized and excited about financial risk management. Although we cannot even dream about what the specifics of financial risk management might be 5 years from now, much less 20 years from now, we are highly confident that it will be dynamic, challenging, and full of potential for those creative and risk-loving enough to take it on.

About the Authors

Brendan Chard, CFA, FRM

Brendan is a risk management expert with significant experience in the energy industry. Having worked in trading, corporate strategy development, and portfolio optimization for a multinational energy conglomerate, he has a deep understanding of the unique challenges faced by companies involved in the energy sector.

Rick Nason, PhD, CFA

Rick is an international consultant and founding partner with RSD Solutions Inc. and an associate professor of finance at Dalhousie University in Halifax, Nova Scotia, Canada. He has advised and developed programs on valuation, risk measurement, risk management, and risk strategy for major global corporations, international financial institutions, government agencies, and several academic institutions with global reach.

Index

OTHER TITLES IN OUR FINANCE AND FINANCIAL MANAGEMENT COLLECTION

John A. Doukas, Old Dominion University, Editor

- *Tips & Tricks for Excel-Based Financial Modeling: A Must for Engineers & Financial Analysts, Volume II* by M. A. Mian
- *The Anti-Bubbles: Opportunities Heading into Lehman Squared and Gold's Perfect Storm* by Diego Parrilla
- *Applied International Finance Volume II, Second Edition: International Cost of Capital and Capital Budgeting* by Thomas J. O'Brien
- *Welcome to My Trading Room, Volume I: Basics to Trading Global Shares, Futures, and Forex - Foundation of Trading* by Jacques Magliolo
- *Hypocrisy of the African Public Finance Management Framework: The Case of Malawi* by Kamudoni Nyasulu
- *Welcome to My Trading Room, Volume II: Basics to Trading Global Shares, Futures, and Forex: Create Your Own Brokerage* by Jacques Magliolo
- *Welcome to My Trading Room, Volume III: Basics to Trading Global Shares, Futures, and Forex–Advanced Methodologies and Strategies* by Jacques Magliolo
- *Enterprise Risk Management in a Nutshell* by Dennis Cox
- *Global Mergers and Acquisitions, Second Edition: Combining Companies Across Borders, Volume II* by Abdol S. Soofi
- *Competing in Financial Markets: How to Play With the Best of Them* by Philip Cooper

Announcing the Business Expert Press Digital Library

Concise e-books business students need for classroom and research

This book can also be purchased in an e-book collection by your library as

- *a one-time purchase,*
- *that is owned forever,*
- *allows for simultaneous readers,*
- *has no restrictions on printing, and*
- *can be downloaded as PDFs from within the library community.*

Our digital library collections are a great solution to beat the rising cost of textbooks. E-books can be loaded into their course management systems or onto students' e-book readers.
The **Business Expert Press** digital libraries are very affordable, with no obligation to buy in future years. For more information, please visit **www.businessexpertpress.com/librarians**. To set up a trial in the United States, please email **sales@businessexpertpress.com**.

www.ingramcontent.com/pod-product-compliance
Lightning Source LLC
Chambersburg PA
CBHW050106210326
41519CB00015BA/3843